Gifts from Our
GRANDMOTHERS

Gifts from Our
GRANDMOTHERS

edited by
CAROL DOVI

foreword by
Anna Eleanor Roosevelt

Crown Publishers
NEW YORK

Published by Crown Publishers, New York, New York. Member of the Crown Publishing Group.

Random House, Inc. New York, Toronto, London, Sydney, Auckland
www.randomhouse.com

Crown is a trademark and the Crown colophon is a registered trademark of Random House, Inc.

Printed in the United States of America

DESIGN BY LYNNE AMFT

Library of Congress Cataloging-in-Publication Data

Gifts from our grandmothers / edited by Carol Dovi.
1. Grandmothers—Miscellanea. 2. Grandparent and child—Miscellanea.
I. Dovi, Carol.
HQ759.9.L475   2000
306.874'5—dc21   99-41285

ISBN 0-609-60488-0

10 9 8 7 6 5 4 3 2 1

First Edition

For my grandmothers,

Frances Dovi, for her steadfast and unconditional love

Sabina Vigilante, for modeling courage in the face of challenges

And my parents,

Frances and Santino Dovi, who taught me to find the humor in life and instilled in me values that continue to serve me well.

CONTENTS

FOREWORD

Anna Eleanor Roosevelt

I realized at a young age that my grandmother, Eleanor Roosevelt, wasn't an "ordinary" grandmother. When she visited our family in California, often as a stopover on business, we couldn't just pick her up at the airport. There were always lots of people, cameras, and activity around her.

My schoolmates also helped teach me that my grandmother was different. I attended school in Pasadena and held the distinction of being the only child in the class who hailed from a Democratic rather than a Republican family. During the McCarthy years, I overheard classmates call my grandmother a "pinko." I knew my grandmother liked blue, so I didn't understand this "pinko" comment. I also didn't know why students talked about *my* grandmother. As the years passed, I better understood their comments. My hurt feelings were gradually replaced by an understanding that my grandmother had committed herself to a public life, and people chose to respond to her in different ways. To me she was an amazing person, a great presence to whom I felt a close connection.

Grandmère, as we grandchildren called her, was purposeful and always working. A wide variety of people constantly surrounded her. When I visited her as a child, however, I remember how she listened to me. She would tilt her head to one side and lean forward, as she was slightly deaf. She wanted to make sure she heard what I said. Many people awaited her attention and yet she focused on me. This simple attentiveness gave me the sense that I was important even while I observed her masterfully balancing and managing the commotion of family and important worldly matters.

I was fortunate also to have another grandmother. My maternal grandmother grew up on a farm in Wisconsin. She was a diaper-changing, cookie-baking grandmother. Granny loved to tell stories, make jokes, and play games. She taught me about quiet strength in the face of hardship and the power of a sense of humor. She, too, gave me an unconditional love.

I found myself using what I had learned from Grandmère and Granny in raising my own two children, now nineteen and twenty-two. I welcomed them in the midst of my work; I helped them to be comfortable with people different from themselves; I urged them to cultivate an interest in the world; and I let them know they were wonderful.

Grandmother can be a generic term. I know Grandmère served in the role of supporter, teacher, and guide to many all over the world, as did the older mentors whose stories are shared in this collection.

Women of various races and religions, backgrounds and ideologies, appear in this anthology. Some are more worldly, as Grandmère was, some are more like Granny, whose own world was a warm destination for us. Each woman is extraordinary in her own way. Their stories demonstrate that unconditional love encourages us to grow, explore, and create authentic lives. They teach us that unconditional love and acceptance are the greatest gifts we have to give.

INTRODUCTION

Chicago's O'Hare airport provided the birthplace for *Gifts from Our Grandmothers*. While waiting for a flight back to Denver, I noticed a woman carrying a book that appeared to be entitled *Bubbies,* the Yiddish word for grandmothers. What a wonderful idea, I thought, a book about grandmothers. My own grandmother, whom I greatly admired, came to mind. I watched the woman approach, eager to write down the exact title and author. When I could read the title clearly, I realized that I had mistaken a spy novel for a book about grandmothers.

That phantom grandmother book stayed with me as my fortieth birthday approached at warp speed, complete with a sense of general discontent. It occurred to me that I needed some guidance as I moved into the second half of my life. I began to write about my Nanny Dovi. The more I wrote about my grandmother, the more I realized that her life provided the guidance that I sought. I began to ask other women to share their grandmother stories.

It was an honor to receive these stories. Writers often shared the desire to see their special grandmother honored in print. One author wrote: ". . . you have helped me communicate a message to my grandmother that I often feared she would never receive. I would like to thank you regardless of whether you accept the manuscript or not. Besides, my grandmother will think it's the best piece of writing she has read in a long time!"

The women remembered in this book used their wisdom to make someone's life a little better, not only through tangible acts of kindness, but through their attitudes of acceptance and caring. They knew the world could be changed one young heart at a time. Contributor Michelle Courtney Berry expressed this feeling in a note attached to her story. She wrote, "I loved my grandmother immensely. Although she died when I was still young, her memories resound within me—clanging bells that remind me to breathe and dream." May these stories inspire you to do the same.

The
CREATIVE
SPIRIT

LOSHAGABOO

Anne Harding Woodworth

s a child, I had my own language—Loshagaboo (lö'-shä-gä-boo'). My brothers and sisters tried speaking it, but never caught on. There was only one person who ever came close to communicating with me in Loshagaboo—my grandmother Nance.

Nance claimed perfect pitch and a well-placed diaphragm, two attributes that had her on her way to an operatic stardom that was never to be. Perhaps it was this unfulfilled dream of hers that contributed to the bond between her and me. Certainly she knew I had my sights set beyond New Jersey. All I knew for sure in those days was that she could belt out Loshagaboo operas better than any diva around.

We always performed after dinner with my large family around the table, looking on. The melody started with her. It was a thin, sweet hum, barely audible. It evolved into a mixture of tune and vowels and consonants that slithered into genuine Loshagaboo.

One night our opera was about travel (in Loshagaboo, that's *neluri*). I picked up on the tune, lamenting that I would *ploonay* (never) see the *kratag pomul* (world) at the rate I was going. Nance assured me I would, predicting *neluri* far and wide for me. I would speak many languages and meet many people of other cultures. I liked hearing all that, but my pessimism about how I was going to do this was consummate. "*Ploonay*," I answered her passionately in a soprano. "I won't ever see the *kratag pomul. Ploonay! Ploonay!*" I swooned. The family mistook my misery for entertainment.

Agnes Barrows

Only Nance understood my despair. She stood up. Fourteen eyes watched her. Her round soft face set itself into an uncharacteristic dignity, as she pulled her chin up, puffed out her diaphragm, heaved her chest full, and gracefully placed one hand into the other on her bosom.

A clear, full note streamed out of her throat, as she began her aria with such tenderness that she took me—perhaps all of us—away with her to her private land of talented and beautiful women, handsome tenors, and lavish sets, to a distant stage, one of differences in lessons and words and thoughts and syllables, of exotic tastes and sauces and oils. Looking around the table, she sang about *shoonaga* (arrogance) of people who expect everyone to know English; and about the *shetoominoo* (necessity) of learning other languages for real understanding among the peoples of the world. Then, turning to me, she sang that I had to believe in the *shanagaboo extolen walinen* (power of the broadening spirit), and she ended in a prophesying cadence: that we should all believe in that power and act on it.

Nance's "prophesy" became my reality. I did get out of New Jersey. I learned Italian, French, and modern Greek. I lived and worked in Rome, Athens, and Frankfurt. Now I live in Washington, D.C., which by its very nature is filled with people from all over the world.

Nance fostered this spirit in me. She knew that getting outside the familiar was a way of discovering oneself. She knew how to tell me this in my own language—better yet, how to sing it to me.

The End (Foon)

ANNE HARDING WOODWORTH'S BOOK OF POETRY, *GUIDE TO GREECE AND BACK*, WAS PUBLISHED IN ATHENS. SHE HAS LIVED IN GREECE AND GERMANY AND TRAVELS IN ITALY EVERY YEAR. ANNE, FIFTY-FIVE, IS THE EDITOR OF THE ANTHOLOGY *SOCCER ZONES: WRITINGS OUT OF AMERICAN SOCCER*.

WE HAD A POEM

Caroline K. Downs

 looked forward to poetry at Grandma's house. After the family greeting and coffee and food, when Grandma had time, we had a poem. As my body grew, my listening position shifted from her lap to her footstool to a chair pulled alongside her rocker. Grandma's position in her rocker remained the same all those years as she read from her little red poetry book.

She started our ritual by asking if I had time to hear a poem that she thought I would like. The question delighted me because I felt like she cherished my opinion. When I consented, she'd hunt for the old schoolhouse book through her special cabinet, its glass doors and four crowded shelves forbidden to children. Once it was located, she laid the volume on her knees while she settled reading glasses on her nose. Then she opened the book to lie flat in her left palm. She turned pages one by one with her right hand, pausing to run her work-worn fingers from top to bottom down the center of each page.

She searched in this manner for the poem she wanted me to hear. I scanned the others, too, and tried to read at the speed of her fingertips, tantalized by glimpses of the words. Finally, she would locate the day's selection and read it over to herself once, her silence punctuated with "hmmmph's" or "mmm-hmmm's," while I tried not to wriggle. After clearing her throat, she began reading aloud while her fingers traced the lines across the page.

Grandma's face intimidated me as she read: her expression serious, brow puckered in concentration, eyes peering over the top of her glasses between stanzas to see my reaction. But her voice captivated me, held me, carried me as it danced through the poem. She uttered the words in a musical way that never degraded to a singsong tone. Her cadence and phrasing created their own dimension of time that lasted through the final line, and then I'd blink my eyes as if awakening from a dream and ask to hear it again. Sometimes she'd oblige and ask me to read it, or we'd read together.

I felt honored whenever she extended our poetry time and flipped pages back to old favorites; she'd ask if I remembered a certain poem, encouraging me to perform. A simple woodpecker poem I memorized at age two stayed popular with us, joined by James Russell Lowell's ode to Grandma's birthday month of June, and the "Moo-Cow-Moo" by Edmund Vance Cook, which made me laugh until tears ran down my cheeks with the images of ". . . deers on its head . . ." and the "nose spread all over the end of its face." Grandma's eyes always twinkled at my merriment.

My grandmother recognized the power poetry held over me, but I failed for too many years to realize the value of the gift she offered. I grew into young adulthood reading and writing verses away from Grandma, and I bought many books of poetry without considering the source of my desire to own such books.

A complicated set of circumstances led me from a college degree in biology to a middle-school teaching position in language arts. Blessed with a job where I share my passion for books and words with students on a daily basis, I am wise enough now to credit Grandma with sowing the seeds for that passion.

My classroom poetry volumes outshine the school library's collection and overflow the shelves of my bookcase. Classes begin each August with one of my favorite poems about school, and I continue to read poetry throughout the year with my students for the sheer joy of the language, rhythm, and themes. My grandmother wished for no better legacy.

CAROLINE K. DOWNS, THIRTY-THREE, LIVES WITH HER FIREFIGHTER HUSBAND IN WORLAND, WYOMING, WHERE SHE TEACHES SIXTH-GRADE LANGUAGE ARTS IN A MIDDLE SCHOOL FULL OF EXUBERANT STUDENTS. WHEN SHE MANAGES TO FIND SPARE TIME, SHE WRITES AND BAKES AND WALKS HER TWO LABRADOR RETRIEVERS.

OF GRANDMOTHERS AND GOOD QUALITY MATERIAL

Mary Byrd Micou Martin

very year in the late summer or early fall, my grandmother Miss Jane visited her sister Sally Page in the Valley of Virginia. Both she and Aunt Sally loved sewing, and during Miss Jane's visits to the Valley, it became a custom to make the long trip to the Crompton textile mill in Danville and bring back yards and yards of corduroy. Back home, as she and my mother and I looked over the colors and discussed patterns, Miss Jane would rub a piece of fabric between thumb and forefinger with satisfaction and say, "This is good quality material."

Miss Jane was slender, composed, reserved, and stylish in her way, wry and dry in her wit. She wore only blue (mostly navy—her favorite) or black or gray. Sometimes with pearls, always with shoes and dark hose that matched. A *lady,* folks said. I don't ever, ever remember my grandmother being loud. Or angry. My mother says she could be extremely angry—but that's her story to tell, not mine. I surely don't doubt that Miss Jane had an iron will. That's a phrase of my mother's.

Jane Byrd Johnson McLaurine

Before she married our grandfather, Miss Jane was a schoolteacher in small places with names like Jetersville and Amelia. I was a teacher, too, for many years, and my sister is still a very good one. It's a profession, I like to think, that draws independent thinkers, and in our family strong-minded women have never been in short supply. I do believe now that Miss Jane taught my sister and me by example some of the traits of a good educator. She listened without prejudging, chuckled often (although never too loudly), and said honestly what she thought but said it kindly.

My mother was her only daughter, and after my grandfather died and the farm was sold, she came to our small town to live with us. She was there when our little sister was born five years later. When she died at 105, she had lived with my parents in that same small town for forty years, no more than a hundred miles from the farm called Cherry Hill where she was born.

After she came to live with us, Miss Jane's three widowed sisters—Aunt Sally, Aunt Mattie, and Lizzie-Mama—would visit fairly often. Each day after lunch, Miss Jane and the visiting sister would repair to her bedroom for an afternoon rest. They'd lower the shades, lie on the bed, cross their ankles, fold their hands at their waists, and talk and laugh in well-modulated tones for an hour or two. They never ran out of talk.

My brother, sister, and I all have memories of conversations with Miss Jane in her room, where usually we'd sprawl on her bed or sit cross-legged on the old trunk while she sat in the rocking chair. She had time to be interested in what we were interested in: our friends, our clothes, the drama of our daily lives.

In the fifties, when pegged pants—those trousers with narrow, tapering legs—were the thing, my brother and his friends, wearing their fifties buzz-cuts with false bravado, would shuffle up the stairs carrying their new slacks to Miss Jane's room, and our little grandmother, in her seventies and wearing her navy-and-pearls, would peg those pants. Although she had defined her own style years earlier, she was a good seamstress and took a keen interest in what, according to the magazines, "they" were wearing.

The summer before I went to college, in 1958, her bedroom was awash with woolens, corduroys, and plaids: Miss Jane and I pored over the *Mademoiselle* college issue, and she and my mother and I planned my wardrobe. She would have laughed at the idea that appearances are unimportant; function without pleasing form was, for her, a waste of perfectly good material.

From the simplest of materials but those of good quality, she created a life that appeared seamless in its composition—and quite beautiful. Without raising her voice, without saying much at all, my grandmother taught me what I needed to know: that I was good quality material and what I created of the fabric was up to me.

MARY BYRD MICOU MARTIN IS A NATIVE VIRGINIAN AND RECENTLY RETIRED AFTER THIRTY-ONE YEARS IN ARLINGTON, VIRGINIA, PUBLIC SCHOOLS. SHE AND HER HUSBAND HAVE TWO GROWN SONS AND STILL LIVE IN ARLINGTON, WHERE SHE NOW WRITES.

MAKING

Gail Sosinsky Wickman

s a child, I never thought my grandmother's hands would stop. They knitted, crocheted, quilted, sewed. At times, her hands seemed to have a life of their own. They embroidered fine stitches while my grandmother carried on lively conversations. They created patterned and beaded necklaces when she seemed half-asleep.

She created to sell; she created to give. She shunned idleness not for fear that quiet hands would be the devil's workshop. She created because her hands demanded usefulness, because her hands desired beauty and pattern and order. To my grandmother, life and action were one.

As she aged, her hands sought simpler tasks, more suited to cataracts and arthritis. And when her making hands were finally still, I realized that these hands were my inheritance.

I see them daily as I embroider my mother's Christmas gift, sew a princess costume for my daughter, or mend the world's most precious teddy bear for my son. The project bag is ever present in my living room, bemusing my husband, who knows we can afford to buy the gifts we give.

Making is my comfort. Cloth against chaos. Immortality in a pillowcase. The patterns of life shaped in embroidery floss. Creativity given substance.

When I touch my grandmother's lone-star quilt, my hands—her hands—become the hands of all women, battling decay and anonymity with a needle and thread. As each stitch connects top to bottom, fabric to fabric, so those stitches connect me, life to life, love to love.

GAIL SOSINSKY WICKMAN LIVES IN CADOTT, WISCONSIN, WITH HER HUSBAND AND TWO SMALL CHILDREN. SHE HAS A B.A. IN JOURNALISM AND AN M.A. IN ENGLISH LITERATURE. THOUGH SHE IS CURRENTLY AN AT-HOME MOM, SHE HAS WORKED AS A TEACHER, A COPY EDITOR, AND A POLKA BAND GUITARIST.

RAG RUGS

Mary A. Heng

The mortician stood at the church door,
handing out holy cards that had the dates of birth and
death and quotes from saints. The inscription on the
card read: "We have loved her during life,
let us not forget her in death."

ST. AMBROSE

The grandchildren of Caroline Kreifels had no intention of forgetting her.

Three months after her wasting death from Alzheimer's, Grandma's household goods were auctioned off. There were few antiques. But to the forty-two grandchildren, the chipped dishes and mugs in which we'd been served ice cream and root-beer floats were icons of childhood. On a hot July day, we gathered in her yard and gave meaning to the phrase "priceless memories."

The chicken salt and pepper shakers went for $25. A broken cookie jar brought $27.50. The cowbell creamer: $45. A&W Root Beer mugs: $25 each. There was hot bidding on a planter of a deer leaping over a log ($45) and the planter of St. Francis of Assisi, whose "hair" grew when wet ($100).

When they weren't crying, my aunts marveled at the prices. "The funny thing is that Grandma wouldn't have given over five dollars for any of this stuff," Aunt Marilyn said.

A child of the Depression, Caroline Kreifels's life was one of making do, and often, of wringing substance out of nothing, which is how the rag rugs started. She began crocheting during the 1950s, tearing ribbons of cloth from worn shirts and dresses she thought too vibrant for scrubbing floors. Lively colored ovals soon dotted the farmhouse wood floors. Over the years, the rugs spread to the homes of her children and grandchildren.

Like the works of an artist, the rugs didn't appreciate in value until their creator died. While waiting for the bidding to start, we cousins recalled how we hadn't thought much of the rugs we received as young adults, how we'd used them in bathrooms and front hallways until they disintegrated. Now, we held our breaths, like bidders at a Christie's auction.

There were four rugs for sale, all hard used. One had a hole in the middle and was close to becoming what it had always been: rags.

The bidding was keen, and one by one, grandchildren dropped out. Like me, they balked at bidding $50, unable to reconcile the price with the woman who'd turned rags into rugs.

Years before her death, Grandma had tried to teach me the art of rug making. We spent an afternoon ripping dresses into strips and arranging them by color.

"It's hard to find clothes where you get enough color at a time," Grandma said. The full skirts of the '50s had been a boon to her rag rugs.

The going was slow. Then eighty-five, Grandma's knuckles were twisted and swollen with arthritis. She could do only a few knots at a time.

"The best part," she said, "is that when you're done, you've made a pretty rug out of something you would've thrown away." That was the mantra of her life: Make something useful out of nothing.

After Grandma's estate sale, I rummaged in my closet for that unfinished rug. The piece didn't amount to more than a skinny center. At first, my knots were uneven and clumsy compared to Grandma's handiwork, but I kept going.

In the face of paying $50 for a rag rug, I knew what my grandmother would have done. She would have made one herself.

MARY HENG, AN OMAHA REPORTER FOR FIFTEEN YEARS, EARNED HER MASTER'S DEGREE IN ENGLISH FROM KANSAS STATE UNIVERSITY IN 1998. SHE HAS PUBLISHED A SCHOLARLY PIECE ON EARLY CREATIVE NONFICTION AND HAS BEEN A FINALIST IN TWO NATIONAL NONFICTION CONTESTS. SHE RECENTLY ENTERED THE M.F.A. PROGRAM AT THE UNIVERSITY OF MINNESOTA.

BUNNY RABBIT

Phoenix Hunter

n impulsive three-year-old in an eager hurry, I had shoved open the front-hall door and burst into Grandma's apartment above ours. Grandma, hunched over her crocheting in the overstuffed chair by the window, glanced up, her wrinkled moon face attentive. In a nonchalant voice she said, "Did you leave the door open for your bunny rabbit?"

Bunny rabbit? I looked back at the open door and saw a rabbit standing upright on the threshold, cloud white, long ears straight up in expectation, nose twitching.

"Come in, Bunny Rabbit," I said with some irritation. "And close the door." Bunny Rabbit hopped in, closed the door, and scampered to a place near Grandma's chair.

No one else could see Bunny Rabbit. His invisibility to others gave me a feeling of being uniquely special, chosen by him. He talked to me in a dusky voice like Grandma's, and he always listened to me. He accompanied me everywhere, closing doors and helping to set the table for meals (he had his own place and chair.) We spent clear, sunny summer days outdoors together, playing pretend horses or weaving dandelion necklaces or exchanging funny stories. He observed from the sidelines when I played with my neighborhood friends. On rainy autumn or cold winter days, we listened to music in my room, played with my dolls, or watched cartoons together.

My father ignored Bunny Rabbit. My mother asked sometimes where Bunny Rabbit was, and if he'd like something to eat. She didn't mind if he came along with us to the grocery store every Thursday. Grandma asked me about Bunny Rabbit, where he slept (in his own bed at the foot of mine), if he was my best friend (of course), and what he liked to do to pass the time.

On Sunday afternoons, my family often piled into our station wagon for a drive in the country. On Bunny Rabbit's first Sunday drive, we had a full car: my father driving and my mother in front; Grandma and Nanny, my other grandmother, in the backseat; and me, Bunny Rabbit, and my older brother in the far back. Nanny hadn't yet met Bunny Rabbit.

"Where's Bunny Rabbit, dear?" Grandma said

"You have a rabbit?" Nanny said, searching around her feet.

"He's invisible," my brother said, giving me a poke in the arm. "Only crazy people see invisible things."

"Well, at least he's not a bear!" Nanny said.

Bunny Rabbit, sitting near my brother and poking him in the arm, smiled.

"Or a lion," Grandma said. And Bunny Rabbit roared. I giggled. Grandma looked back to me and smiled a knowing cat-smile.

It was that same smile I saw on Grandma's face after my first day of school. I had told her Bunny Rabbit hadn't wanted to go to school again. He hopped out of my life that day. Grandma nodded but said nothing. Her cat-smile told me not to be sad.

At five years old, I couldn't have known that Bunny Rabbit was the first character I would create. Over the years, a long line of "imaginary friends" have come to tell me their stories and to live on the page. Grandma, and her smile, had left the door of my imagination open for them.

PHOENIX HUNTER, FORTY-THREE, IS THE PEN NAME USED BY A MINNESOTA FICTION WRITER FOR HER NONFICTION. SHE HAS PUBLISHED ESSAYS IN NEWSLETTERS AND WORKED AS A FREELANCE COPYWRITER AND EDITOR. AT TIMES, SHE HAS SUPPORTED HER WRITING VOCATION BY WORKING AS AN ADMINISTRATIVE ASSISTANT.

ABUELITA'S BEE

Lori Cardona

y grandmother Inez Rita's home in Spanish Harlem was the big-city haven of my childhood summers. I listened to the sound of Latin rhythms as the neighbors sat out on tenement steps to share their loud enthusiasm for having the workday behind, the night in front, and the music throughout. We'd frequently get up to dance in the middle of snacking on guava, cheese, and crackers, because a radio's song inspired us to twirl around the room while licking our fingers and spilling crumbs. While my Anglo friends spent their summers basking on the Jersey shores, I was learning the subway system from the theater district to Amsterdam Avenue, racing my cousins across a cement playground on 138th Street, and hanging off a third-story fire escape to admire the CCNY students to my left and the lights of

Palisades Park, over the Hudson, to my right. I was filling my lungs and my heart with city sights and city sounds, a world away from the state next door.

Abuelita always seemed to be making something. She created handmade lace, using a complicated system of threads wound over a small decorative box of wooden sticks. She twisted and turned the threads one over the other, until long beautiful strips of lace appeared. Sometimes I stood on a stool as she measured me by finger-lengths to make me nightgowns trimmed in lace. As she crocheted doilies for tabletops, she told me stories of her youth in Puerto Rico.

Away from her, I lived my Catholic-schoolgirl life, biding my time in anticipation of her visits. Every other Saturday, Bus 34 brought my grandmother to my small suburban hometown. She was my roommate on those weekends, the reason I grew up with an extra bed in my room, an empty drawer in my dresser, and grown-up romance "novellas," written in Spanish, lying on the bookcase, next to my dolls.

On her weekends in New Jersey, she played cards with the grown-ups and seemed, almost, to be one of them. But then, as we were lying in our beds, she'd call me to get up and come fix her hair. I'd rush to her bedside and turn on the light. We'd both laugh out loud with the door closed behind us. I untied the dollar bills she'd woven through her gray locks like curlers. In mostly Spanish and a bit of broken English, she'd tell me to just throw them away because she'd have plenty more for the next time she needed a curl. I'd go back to bed and sleep peacefully, with Abuelita's love and dollar bills tucked under my pillow.

My grandmother was seventy-two years old, and I was twelve, when she finally agreed to move into our suburban home. The upstairs attic was transformed from a weak-floored storage space, formerly accessed through a trapdoor in the ceiling, to a two-room apartment with a tiny bathroom at the top of a newly created, carpeted stairway.

In December of 1973, five years after moving in with us, she was taken to the hospital for some routine tests. Within twenty-four hours she was dead. A Catholic church calendar I found in her room documented her daily feelings of discomfort and pain, written in small letters, squeezed in around the preprinted facts of saints and holy days. In the chapel at her funeral, I put on the bracelet I had made for her a year before and which she refused to ever take off. I promised to wear it forever. I cried for her, wrote a song for her, took her memory, and stored it in my heart.

Many years later, I stood in the lobby of a museum in Miami, listening to an artist describe her craft. The artist found antique textiles and incorporated the lace, doilies, and imagined life stories of their creators into large oil and acrylic paintings on canvas. I suddenly realized the extent of my grandmother's talents. I remembered all the beautiful crocheted items she made for everyone who asked. I grieved the fact that I no longer owned a piece of her handiwork. I wondered to myself who did own a piece of my grandmother's history.

I remembered that my grandmother had crocheted a doily for the window in the front door of a childhood friend's home. Their last name started with a *B,* so they asked her to crochet a doily with a *B* in the middle. When I saw the finished product and noted that the *B* in the middle was in the shape of a bee, the insect, I attributed it to a language barrier. But then I realized it was her own artistic expression and a stroke of genius. I have recovered a few precious pieces of her loving handiwork. To my great joy, I found Abuelita's bee, a reminder of talent overlooked and great lessons in love.

LORI CARDONA, FORTY-ONE, IS OF PUERTO RICAN AND MEXICAN HERITAGE. SHE HOLDS A B.A. IN PSYCHOLOGY AND A GRADUATE DEGREE IN HUMAN DEVELOPMENT. SHE CURRENTLY RESIDES IN FORT LAUDERDALE, FLORIDA, AND WORKS AS AN ADMINISTRATOR OF A MENTAL-HEALTH PROGRAM.

NOTES FROM NONA

Antoinette Harrington

"Che-Ge-li-da-Ma-ni-na,"
seven syllables sung on one note.
Rodolfo, the tenor,
takes Mimi's tiny cold hand in his.
The audience sobs.
I chill as the song takes me back . . .

Nona stands at the cast-iron stove,
her voice softly humming the seven notes,

her swollen, tired hands dipping the
chicken into the seasoned breading,
then into the crackling, hot oil.

All the while she sings softly,
"Che-Ge-li-da-Ma-ni-na."
Her hands teach the toils of reality,
her voice teaches the music of escape.

lthough I first heard her sing this aria over fifty years ago, I see her clearly and still know the sound of her voice. I was seven when Nona took charge of me. My parents worked, so every day after school, I'd walk an extra block to Nona's house, where I'd stay until my parents came home. I'd climb the twenty-one steps to the second floor and wait, my ear pressed against the door to hear her voice humming another aria.

Nona decided I would take piano lessons, although my feet could not reach the pedals. Each day I'd practice, searching out the melodies to songs Nona hummed. Then I'd hear her call to me, *"Scales, Antoinette, practice the scales."* And the Do-Re-Mi's would begin. I hated them. They weren't music. When I thought she was too busy to pay attention, I'd try picking out songs, and again she'd admonish, *"Scales, Antoinette, scales."* The music lived in my soul, but I could never get my fingers to create the sounds I wanted to hear.

Blind from diabetes, Nona rarely left the house. The radio provided her link with the outside world. During the summer months, I would sleep over. Our mornings began with Arthur Godfrey (whom she loved until he fired Julius La Rosa), followed by the trials of Helen Trent and then Ma Perkins. Later, as she cleaned the house, Nona would share her life with me, stories of living in Europe near the Adriatic Sea. At night, she took her place in her favorite armchair, and I'd snuggle on the floor between her knees. Together, we'd listen to *The Shadow, Inner Sanctum,* or *Fibber McGee and Molly.* Afterward, she'd tell me the sad stories behind the operas—of Rodolfo and Mimi's tragic love, Violetta's dreadful illness, and the horrible plight of Aida and Radames. I loved them all and dreamed that I would someday have the talent to create music as beautiful as the music she shared with me.

Fifty years later, I still cannot create the music; but earlier this year, my daughter took her place on a concert stage. In her rich, strong soprano voice, she became Mimi, responding to Rodolfo, as he clutched her tiny cold hand in his. Thank you, Nona— the music lives on.

ANTOINETTE HARRINGTON, A NATIVE OF CHICAGO, RESIDES WITH HER HUSBAND, DAN, IN DOWNERS GROVE, ILLINOIS. THEY HAVE TWO COLLEGE-AGE CHILDREN, DANIEL AND KELLI. SHE HAS BEEN WRITING FOR FIFTEEN YEARS AND HAS PUBLISHED POETRY AND NONFICTION.

Helen Christine Sullivan

Erminia Nakicen

NANA'S STORIES

Mary Quattlebaum

ith her stories, Nana was like some fairy-tale girl with a magical tongue. You never knew what metaphorical rose or snake might fall from her lips, but you could be sure she'd hold you spellbound on those rainy days or winter nights when she'd draw up her rocker, take up her knit-ting, and start into telling. My three brothers, three sisters, and I would huddle round openmouthed to hear her. Cautionary tales, quotes, bits of wisdom, stories from her Irish-lass days in a New England mill town—Nana never ran dry. And she was never one to draw a dusty drape between fiction and fact. She loved to take a plain-cotton kind of event and make it fancy with frou-frou and lace.

She's gone now; dead for twenty-one years, but not a day goes by that I don't think of her. Her rambunctiousness is in my sister, who carries her middle name, her good humor in the one who bears her first. And of course, her stories get told and retold as we sip our tea, white and sweet and hot, the way she took it, and bend the ears of any listening child. Being a shy type, I had to take up the pen to get my own stories told; and in the books I write for kids, she often creeps—or leaps—right in. Her way of telling, the sound of her voice, have shaped the way I write. I'm grateful that it's so.

MARY QUATTLEBAUM, THIRTY-NINE, IS THE AUTHOR OF SEVEN CHILDREN'S BOOKS. *JAZZ, PIZZAZZ, AND THE SILVER THREADS* AND *UNDERGROUND TRAIN* FEATURE OLDER WOMEN BASED ON HER GRANDMOTHER. SINCE 1986 MARY HAS DIRECTED ARTS PROJECT RENAISSANCE, A CREATIVE- AND AUTOBIOGRAPHY-WRITING PROGRAM FOR OLDER ADULTS.

SNAPSHOTS

Karyn D. Kedar

"hen you come to visit, will you bring me pictures of my grandmothers?" I asked my parents who were planning a trip to Chicago. I had become curious about these women whom I never knew. I wanted to give my children a sense of their history, their story. I believe that our lives are a collection of stories and songs to be told and hummed by the generations that live when we are gone. It was time I told the stories of my grandmothers.

When my parents arrived, there were a flurry of hugs and kisses and presents for the children. My father pulled an envelope out of his suitcase and handed it to me. There were the pictures I had asked for. He had handed me my gift, images of my unknown past.

I first looked at the picture of Mum Mum, my father's mother who died when I was young. My only memories of her were of the Alzheimer patient she had become. I study the picture, recognizing the lamp that now stands in my living room, the chair, the photos, and then I see the desk. Like a flash I remember the desk as it stood in my father's den. It was a great mystery in my house. Ours was a home without locks; no locked doors, bathrooms, emotions. Except the desk: The third drawer from the top

Evangeline
Dion Schwartz

Nellie Weisman

was always locked. In this drawer were my grandmother's manuscripts, poems, plays, and thoughts. Over the years I would ask my father to unlock the drawer and let me touch the pages, read the words, feel their power. But he would usually say, "No, not now." A couple years ago he took my oldest daughter into the room. They closed the door and Daddy shared the holy pages with her. Neither of them ever revealed what transpired.

I looked at the picture again. I studied Mum Mum's face for a clue, any clue as to who she really was. What if I marched into my father's house and demanded the key to the drawer? I could read the pages of her imagination, understand the workings of her mind. "I could know you," I whispered to the black-and-white image.

But I already know you. As I gaze into your eyes and I see my own reflection staring back. "We inherit souls as well as genes," I imagine you saying. I look at your picture, and I realize that I have inherited the soul of the poet, the soul of defiance, the soul of strength.

Suddenly I glanced at the picture of my other grandmother. I have no name for her. She died before I could speak. I see her lifting me in the air, and I seem to her hear her Polish accent sing, *"Tance, tance, madele"* ("Dance, dance, little girl"). It's the song my mother sang to my children when they were young.

Mum Mum is right. I have inherited more than their genes. I shall dance and I shall sing. I will study the pictures and tell the story as I live it in my soul. And as I age, the mystery will be revealed. Without knowing the details of their daily lives, their legacy lives on in the twists and turns of my life as I am urged to live by their dreams for me.

RABBI KARYN D. KEDAR, FORTY-TWO, IS THE AUTHOR OF *GOD WHISPERS: STORIES OF THE SOUL, LESSONS OF THE HEART.* SHE IS THE DIRECTOR OF THE CHICAGO AND GREAT LAKES REGION OF THE UNION OF AMERICAN HEBREW CONGREGATIONS. KARYN RESIDES IN A CHICAGO SUBURB WITH HER HUSBAND AND THREE CHILDREN.

AND THEN THE MONSTER ATE THE PRINCESS . . .

Jennifer Rachel Baumer

he lamp light in the living room of the Santa Monica apartment was low. My grandfather's memorial proved more a celebration of his life than a mourning of our loss. By now, my Grandmother's breathing was no longer easy, her eyes were tired, her hands hurting, and she no doubt wished we'd all go away and let her rest.

I sat beside her on the gold-and-velvet monstrosity of a couch and slipped her a note in fourteen-year-old writing.

"Dear Grandmother. How are you? Fine, I hope. I am fine. Love, Jennifer."

"Dear Kid," she wrote back, "I am fine. How are you? Love, me."

"Dear Grandmother. I said 'I am fine' already. Are you? Love, Kid."

"I did too! Hush!"

Our notes became sillier and our handwriting worse, and the two of us giggled like schoolgirls or best friends. All the adults were in the kitchen.

It seemed logical to communicate in writing to my silver-haired grandmother while sitting directly beside her. She was the one who started me playing with words.

I dictated my first poem to my mother at age three, and she dutifully wrote it down. She must have sent a copy to my grandmother because by the time I was four, she was sending me story beginnings to continue.

"The princess in the woods came around a tree and she *saw* . . ., *you* go on with it." And of course she saw a monster who devoured her whole. I sent that back and waited for accolades. She continued the story sometime later, and a little to my dismay wrote, . . . "and the prince came along and killed the monster and saved the princess and they all lived happily ever after." The next partial story came and the next, until at age seven I wrote my own comic books and by high school I was writing novels.

And letters. All those letters. "Thank you for the birthday check. I bought a new album with it. Here are some of the lyrics." And she'd always write back that she wished she could be with me so we could listen to Bruce Springsteen together. I always knew she was making that up, but I wished it too.

She burned her stories when they were returned after being submitted for publication. The woman who spent untold hours writing stories to go with magazine cutouts for her six grandchildren, burned any story so lousy, so poorly written, that it was rejected on the first time out. Her few surviving stories sit in a special folder in my writing room, labeled *Grandmother's Stories*. They are dated and precious and the best encouragement I could ever ask for.

JENNIFER RACHEL BAUMER HAS BEEN WRITING SINCE AGE THREE AND HOPES SHE IS DOING BETTER MATERIAL THAN THE ORIGINAL CEMENT-MIXER POEM.

WISE
COUNSEL

PAYING ATTENTION

Julia Cameron

lora and fauna reports," I used to call the long winding letters from my grandmother. "The forsythia is starting, and this morning I saw my first robin. . . . The roses are holding even in this heat. . . . My Christmas cactus is getting ready. . . ."

I followed my grandmother's life like a long home movie: a shot of this and a shot of that, spliced together with no pattern that I could ever see. "Dad's cough is getting worse. . . . The little Shetland looks like she'll drop her foal early. . . . Joanne is back in the hospital at Anna. . . . We named the new boxer Trixie, and she likes to sleep in my cactus bed—can you imagine?"

I could imagine. Her letters made that easy. Life through Grandma's eyes was a series of small miracles: the wild tiger lilies under the cottonwoods in

June; the quick lizard scooting under the gray river rock she admired for its satiny finish. Her letters clocked the seasons of the year and her life. She lived until she was eighty, and the letters came until the very end. When she died, she went as suddenly as her Christmas cactus had; here today, gone tomorrow. She left behind her letters and her husband of sixty-two years. Her husband, my grandfather Daddy Howard, an elegant rascal with a gambler's smile and a loser's luck, had made and lost several fortunes, the last of them permanently. He drank them away, gambled them away, tossed them away the way she threw crumbs to her birds. He squandered life's big chances the way she savored the small ones. "That man," my mother would say.

My grandmother lived with that man in tiled Spanish houses, in trailers, in a tiny cabin halfway up a mountain, in a railroad flat, and finally, in a house made out of ticky-tacky where they all looked just the same. "I don't know how she stands it," my mother would say, furious with my grandfather for some new misadventure. She meant she didn't know why.

The truth is, we all knew how she stood it. She stood it by standing knee-deep in the flow of life and paying close attention.

My grandmother was gone before I learned the lesson her letters were teaching: Survival lies in sanity, and sanity lies in paying attention. Yes, her letters said, "Dad's cough is getting worse"; "we have lost the house"; "there is no money and no work, but the tiger lilies are blooming"; "the lizard has found that spot of sun"; "the roses are holding even in this heat."

My grandmother knew what a painful life had taught her: Success or failure, the truth of a life really has little to do with its quality. The quality of life is in proportion always to the capacity for delight. The capacity for delight is the gift of paying attention.

JULIA CAMERON, THE AUTHOR OF THE *ARTIST'S WAY* AND *VEIN OF GOLD*, HAS BEEN A WORKING ARTIST FOR MORE THAN TWENTY YEARS.

THE FABRIC OF DIVERSITY

Deborah Shouse

ong before there was diversity training, my grandmother made me dolls from other countries. She made them with cotton, colorful seconds from Filene's Basement. Grandma was a child-sized woman, with a birdlike brittleness, yet she was strong enough to hold her own with the bargain-hunting crowds. Her own "diversity training" had included Russian pogroms; New York City sweatshops; postcanal life of Colon, Panama; and now, after her husband died and her children left home, living in an Irish and Italian neighborhood near Boston. At Filene's, she found black cotton for the African doll, white for the Swiss, red for the Indian, brown for the

South American, and the bright scraps for their native costumes.

Every holiday, I received a battered box populated with a new country, the doll's eyes a bright thread that never stopped looking at me; the mouth, a cherry stitching that always kept its smile. I slept next to the wall, with my collection of dolls beside me. France cuddled next to Germany; Russia nestled China; and America leaned on Japan, an international line of different skins and customs, held together by the same fabrics: cotton . . . and love.

DEBORAH SHOUSE OFTEN THINKS OF HER GRANDMOTHER, WHO WAS A MAGICAL COMBINATION OF HUMOR, FRAGILITY, LOVE, AND STRENGTH. DEBORAH IS COAUTHOR OF *ANTIQUING FOR DUMMIES* AND HAS CONTRIBUTED TO MAGAZINES SUCH AS *MS, WOMAN'S DAY, FAMILY CIRCLE,* AND *READER'S DIGEST.*

Lena Barnett

LIFE LESSONS
Lee Heffner

he came to Chicago in 1921, with beautiful red hair and a sixth-grade education. Both were good enough for AT&T. She spoke of Ma Bell with reverence, like she was a grand old lady who had handpicked my grandmother to sit by her side. She worked as a night cleaner until her retirement forty-seven years later. She taught me pride in my work.

She took me to my first movie when I was two. I knew Bette Davis better than my aunt. We saw everything. She would explain the parts I didn't understand, and we would talk about what had made us laugh and cry. She taught me art appreciation.

She divorced my grandfather after thirty-two years of marriage. Police did not intervene in domestic disputes in 1952. There were no restraining orders or refuge houses. She left everything behind and moved into a fourth-floor walk-up with two rooms. She taught me courage.

She met a widower, from the old country. They fell in love and stayed married until his death thirty years later. It was a happy, loving, sexual relationship. She taught me to never make the same mistake twice.

Mary Ruth
Davidson

She acted as the quizmaster for an immigrant coworker studying for the citizenship exam. She knew fewer answers than her pal. She called, fretting, and asked if she could be deported. I assured her that she could not since she had been born in the United States. She taught me the importance of education.

She spent every Saturday with me. We played Sorry, War, and Old Maid while watching *The Buster Brown Show*. She would make a special dinner, followed by vanilla ice cream covered in Hershey's chocolate syrup. It is still my favorite comfort food. She taught me joy in simple pleasures.

At eighty-seven, when she was being released from the hospital, we waited an hour and a half for an ambulance to take her home. When the second hour struck on her retirement watch, she lost her patience. "Go out front and hail me a cab!" She taught me independence.

She died six years later. She taught me grace.

LEE HEFFNER, FIFTY-ONE, IS THE FIRST, AND SOME SAY THE ONLY, GRANDCHILD OF MARY RUTH DAVIDSON. SHE IS A SUCCESS IN GENERALLY ACCEPTED TERMS. AT A DEEPER LEVEL, SHE IS A SUCCESS BECAUSE SHE LEARNED HER GRANDMOTHER'S LESSONS WELL.

YAYA

Andrea Potos

he first five years of my life, my family lived in the duplex apartment above Yaya's on Fifty-second Street in Milwaukee. Her back door was never locked. Every morning I wound down the spiral of shining maple stairs and landed in her kitchen. "Hello, my *koukla*," she'd say, her words wrapping around me like the soft afghans she crocheted. My first question was always: "Do you have any gum or candy, Yaya?" Most often she'd give me a Hershey bar with almonds, or slices of her own toasted bread, slathered with butter and dripping gold through the pores onto my plate. If my timing was just right, I'd get samples of her still-warm Greek cookies— beautiful egg-glazed braids of dough, white crescent moons.

When my family moved across town, it felt like countries away from Yaya.

Three times a day I'd call her. I still remember the number—444-2065. There was welcome in her voice when she heard mine at the other end of the line. I'd tell her about my pet turtle dying under its plastic palm tree, the fancy illustrated edition of *Little Women* I found, or our new, big stainless-steel sink where I scrubbed my hair with Johnson's baby shampoo. Though I could not name it then, my mother was too depressed to hear me, my father too absent. Yaya heard.

The winter I was twenty-five, I spent every Saturday afternoon in Yaya's kitchen —now in a small apartment she and my grandfather moved to after forty-four years in the duplex. I was driven to learn those beloved Greek recipes she'd cooked for the family all those years: the succulently sweet *baklava, kourambeides, melamakarona,* the savory *pasticio, spanokopita, dolmades.* She taught me how to keep the fillo dough from drying out, how to fold the *trigona* so the cheeses would stay tucked inside.

Yaya was never one to preach. Only once she told me: "Don't let your life be childless." For years I'd wavered over the decision to have a child. I was still undecided ten years into my marriage. Could I bear the weight of so much responsibility? Did I really want my life to change?

But I remembered her words.

Five weeks after my daughter was born, Yaya died at the age of eighty-eight. I felt so exposed without her, as if there was nothing between me and the universe. I gradually began to feel the strength and the joy of my own motherhood. I look at my daughter now and realize the love and wisdom that made her possible.

ANDREA POTOS, THIRTY-EIGHT, IS A POET LIVING IN MADISON, WISCONSIN, WITH HER HUSBAND AND DAUGHTER. HER WORK HAS APPEARED IN MANY JOURNALS AND HAS RECENTLY BEEN ANTHOLOGIZED IN *AT OUR CORE: WOMEN WRITING ABOUT POWER* (PAPIER-MACHE PRESS) AND *CLAIMING THE SPIRIT WITHIN* (BEACON PRESS).

A MEASURE OF AGE

Opal Palmer Adisa

she moved slowly
not because she couldn't walk fast
but she had lived long enough
to know no matter the
speed of the river
it will meet the sea

that was her constant comhment
everything in its own time
and no matter how often
I asked how come
she would merely shake her head and
smile

I had to slow down when I was with her
I learned to measure the passing of time

saw it move on its own legs

my grandmother was a study in patience
she allowed no one
to ruffle her calm
and told me to stay away
from people who were always in haste
they are running from themselves
she would caution
pointing to the even-paced rhythm of
nature
she taught me how to study things
slowly   with care
how to detect and relish
the beauty in all

my grandmother made me want to sprint
to become her

she made aging a timeless thing
of immense beauty

but I know
I too will experience
a measure of time

OPAL PALMER ADISA HAS A PH.D. IN ETHNIC STUDIES LITERATURE. SHE HAS TAUGHT AT SAN FRANCISCO STATE UNIVERSITY AND THE UNIVERSITY OF CALIFORNIA, BERKELEY. PRESENTLY SHE IS ASSOCIATE PROFESSOR AND CHAIR OF THE ETHNIC STUDIES PROGRAM AT CALIFORNIA COLLEGE OF ARTS AND CRAFTS. SHE LIVES IN OAKLAND WITH HER THREE CHILDREN.

Edith
Palmer

GIRL, GO GET YOU A FUR

Yolanda Joe

he color of dirty rice and just as spicy, this Louisiana lady was born on the low end with highbrow ideas. A racist society limited life's opportunities and fenced her in; but she leaned on that fence and dreamed of what could be for her daughters to come. This woman was my grandmother Bernice Barnett.

She suffered from a chronic case of "sugar," but as my grandmother would say "there's nothing sweet about it." Sugar is what black people call diabetes.

Diabetes broke my grandmother's body but not her spirit. With her eyesight gone, she used a keen sense of hearing, intuition, touch, and humor to communicate and understand what was going on around her.

My grandmother had more flair than a Mardi Gras fan plus 'tude when it wasn't in vogue for a small-town bayou girl in the 1930s. She loved clothes. Fashion and looking good were her passion. It was born out of girlhood days when she washed sheets for white women; they openly joked that colored girls looked dirty even when they went to church.

My grandmother believed a woman wasn't dressed up if her shoes, bag, and hat didn't match—and oh yes, break that hat down over the eye wouldya pretty please?

Neither age nor disease diminished my grandmother's passion for fashion. After migrating from her hometown of Monroe, Louisiana, to Chicago, a fierce love of furs developed. My grandmother had four furs—full length, three-quarter, a swing, and a stole.

It used to drive her crazy that I lived in Chicago and didn't own a fur. She would wonder out loud, Is it possible? Could I be her grandchild and live in the Windy City with a "good job" and not own a fur? Not able to deny me because I had her features and some of her ways, my grandmother began a running, funny debate with me. The opening round always began with a curl of the lip, a "say that, preacher" hand wave, and the bluesy phrase, "Girl, go get you a fur!"

What follows is a poem packed with points from my grandmother the "furologist." *Bernice, girl, you are loved and you are missed—but no, I still didn't buy that fur!*

For my grandmother

GET YOU A FUR!!!

You mean you in Chicago with cold winds that cut like a knife, out on Rush and other streets, in all that fine lush night life?	*GIRL, GO GET YOU A FUR!!!*
	Do you want your legs to get cold & snap like chicken bones . . .

or get all ashy like raw corn pone?

Do you want your bosom cold as ice
cubes?
or your hips creaking when you walk like
an
old car needing an oil lube?

YOU BETTER GO GET YOU A FUR!!!

Don't you know every black woman
worth her
pepper deserves a fur?
putting up with so much mess and stress
in
our world.

We've gone from nigra gals, to colored
girls,
to Negro women, to black grandmas.

Shoot I've had racism, women-get-
back-ism,

age, & crazy men riding my back . . .
And I'mah here to tell you, it's an easier
load to carry in a fur . . .
even if it's off the rack!

Now don't get me wrong and run out
like some
folks and get something cheap now,
instead of the very best fur later . . .

Silly rabbit coats are for kids . . .
leave Bugs Bunny in the funny papers!

Animal rights, shoot piss on that mink . . .
and all the folks who think more about
his
four legs than they do my two!

Don't you see Auntie, just trying to tell
you
what to do?

GO GET YOU A FUR!!!!

YOLANDA JOE IS A GRADUATE OF YALE UNIVERSITY AND COLUMBIA SCHOOL OF JOURNALISM. SHE IS THE AUTHOR OF THE BLACKBOARD BEST-SELLING BOOK *HE SAY; SHE SAY*. HER NEW NOVEL, *THIS JUST IN,* WILL BE PUBLISHED IN MARCH BY DOUBLEDAY, AND HER FIRST ARDELLA GARLAND MYSTERY, *DETAILS AT TEN*, WILL DEBUT IN SEPTEMBER FROM SIMON & SCHUSTER.

KEEP THE RING

Kimberly O'Lone

 hen the automatic glass doors at the entrance of the Holland Nursing Home swung open, I hesitated. How could I tell ninety-two-year-old Grandma Perry about my divorce? Only two years after our big wedding, Tom was having an affair with a skinny woman who dyed her hair orange and always wore black because she said she was an artist. I was twenty-seven, and felt that I had failed as a wife, and therefore failed at life. I wouldn't be surprised if Grandma asked for her pink-rose quilt back. I was not worthy of such a family heirloom.

Before I reached Grandma's room, Sally, the activity director, recognized me. "Mrs. Perry is in physical therapy," she said. "You can wait in her room."

Good. I could put off my confession for a few more minutes. As I sat in the green vinyl chair next to Grandma Perry's bed, I stared at her wall calendar from the Daughters of the Eastern Star, the Lady Shriners for whom she was a past High Priestess. It was October 8, 1982. The first seven days of the month had large black X's marked through them. November 12 had a large red circle on it, with the word HOME inside it. Grandma Perry had been living in her little two bedroom house in Riverdale, Illinois, on August 12, when she had broken her hip. Her doctor had told her it would take at least four months to recover. "Then I'm going to be out of here in November," she had said, and it looked like she was going to make it.

An afghan crocheted in variegated blue stripes was folded on Grandma's bed. On the side table was the dark green afghan she was working on. Grandma had started crocheting for the Red Cross at seventy-one. Last year she had earned her pin for twenty years of service. If Grandma could start volunteering at seventy-one, maybe, just maybe, I could rebuild my life.

From the hallway I could hear Grandma's voice. "I'm going to talk to Mrs. Noonan in 107 about coming to bingo. She can't just keep sitting in her room."

"I would appreciate that, Mrs. Perry. She listens to you," said Sally.

When she saw me, Grandma wheeled herself into the room and reached out for my hand. "How are you, dear?" she said.

"Not so good. I'm divorcing Tom," I said, and held my breath. I hadn't meant to just blurt the news out. Grandma was silent. I could feel my heart beating out of my chest. Then Grandma gestured for me to come close to her. She whispered "Did you keep the ring?"

"I did," I said, and laughed.

"Good for you," she said, and patted my shoulder. I pulled my chair closer, and began to tell her all about it.

KIMBERLY O'LONE IS FORTY-ONE YEARS OLD, AND HOLDS A MASTER'S IN PUBLIC ADMINISTRATION FROM THE UNIVERSITY OF ILLINOIS AT CHICAGO. SHE AND HER HUSBAND, JIM, ARE THE PROUD PARENTS OF ELIZABETH AND ROSEMARY JOYCE.

Evelyn Perry

Angeline Potter

LEGACY FROM ANGELINE

Nancy Angeline Potter

efore recordings and videos, my grandmother Angeline Potter had faded into one small faint portrait in a gold frame. But these facts about her I know.

Born in 1835, she grew up on a tiny Rhode Island farm. The whole rushing nineteenth century would betray such farms. Courageous neighbors boarded wagon trains and headed west. The successful new textile mills had already destroyed hand weaving, which had supported the family for centuries. Angeline said good-bye to formal education after she won the last Reward of Merit in the one-room school.

In 1862, she fell in love and married a young farmer, who marched south

66

and was dead in Virginia within the year. According to family stories, she hitched up a team, collected his coffin at the nearest railroad station, and buried him near home. Trying to survive on the small Civil War widow's pension, she worked as a seamstress and milliner in a Providence bonnet shop. My grandfather, a distant cousin, walked in one day and proposed. She accepted immediately and remained permanently grateful for the rescue. He was relatively prosperous, thirty-five years older, and had already outlived two wives. Their only child, my father, was born in 1869.

Angeline was a prudent farm woman, with enduring enthusiasm for reading and for women's suffrage. She bought herself sets of Shakespeare, Dickens, Twain, and Byron, and she also enjoyed novels by Alcott and Stowe, and collected the complete works of Marietta Holley, who wrote satire and humor under the pen name of Josiah Allen's Wife. She subscribed to *Godey's Lady's Book* for the patterns and *Harper's Illustrated* and *Frank Leslie's Monthly* for the news, and then had all the issues bound in half-leather for later rereading. The magazines, her bonnets, and dresses and quilts outlasted her to live now in libraries and textile museums.

When my father had to leave the farm to continue his education, she wrote him an encouraging letter every day throughout school and college, and he kept them for the rest of his life. She was dead by 1898, missing my father's passionate oratorical support of women's suffrage in the state assembly and the passage of the Nineteenth Amendment.

These stories she left me, along with her name; the books; her one piece of good jewelry, a handsome gold necklace she designed for herself; and another incredibly generous legacy. Through a lifetime of small economies, she had managed to save ten thousand dollars. Her will established a small trust fund for the education of any of her grandchildren who might be born. Almost fifty years after her death, that fund sent me to college. And that, truly, made all the difference.

NANCY ANGELINE POTTER, SEVENTY-ONE, IS A PROFESSOR (EMERITA) OF ENGLISH AT THE UNIVERSITY OF RHODE ISLAND. SHE HAS BEEN A FULBRIGHT LECTURER AND HAS PUBLISHED TWO COLLECTIONS OF SHORT STORIES.

CRUSADER

Estelle Peixa

armela Josefa and Paul "Pepper" Guerra, my grandparents, were field-workers in the vineyards, and their children were hired as pickers in season. But Carmela made sure that all the Guerra children finished high school. She worked out of season doing housework in the *patrón*'s home, and even borrowed money once so that her oldest, my papa, could stay in school.

Before there was any thought of a union, the Bartolomes, Italian vintners near our town, were considered good employers. They didn't cheat people, or make picky rules. They got to know their workers. They liked to hire their workers' families, which is how my brother and I came to pick for half days in the summer as soon as we were old enough.

When the grape boycott came, and I joined the protesters who were trying to make the field a better place to work, my grandmother didn't understand. She didn't want me to disrespect the Bartolomes, who had always been good to our family.

"A person should have a rest break," I told her. "A person should have a toilet, a lunchtime. It's dignity, *abuelita*."

"I know about *dignidad*," said Carmela Josefa. "When Papa and I were first married, the women had to go out behind those two old eucalyptus trees in the west field. We would go out there and lift our skirts, right out in the open. We closed our eyes and made our own *dignidad*. And the men, they had honor. They would keep their eyes on the grapes, and they would sing, to give us privacy."

"Sylvia," she said to me, "don't get in with these field-workers, don't get stuck there. You're smart and pretty, *mija*, I want to see you get ahead. Work in a clean place, my baby, where there is a ladies room."

I didn't become a union big shot, but I showed up at the rallies and somehow I got my picture in the paper, sweating and screaming in front of a line of deputies. I didn't want Grandma to see it, but she did. She cut the picture out. She took it to church. She showed everyone the newspaper clipping and said, "That's my granddaughter, my *nieta*, the crusader."

ESTELLE PEIXA, FIFTY-EIGHT, LIVES IN WATSONVILLE, CALIFORNIA. SHE WRITES UNDER THIS PEN NAME, WHICH IS A PORTUGUESE IDIOM MEANING "STARFISH," THE CREATURE THAT REGENERATES FROM DEEP WOUNDS AND CREATES JOY.

GRANDMA AND I GOT AWAY

Rachel Sarah

 "H e was one of those people you'd call a controller," Grandma Ruth says.

I'm sitting on the porch with my eighty-six-year-old grandmother in Fort Dodge, Iowa, the town where she was born and raised. It's been twenty years since I last visited this place, where all roads reach cornfields. The bells at Sacred Heart Church across the street ring twelve times in a row. "I never talked about him with anyone," Grandma says.

For as long as I remember, she has always spoken about Grandpa simply as "he," not Ed. Grandma goes back and forth in her rocking chair, a crossword-puzzle book balanced on one knee. She reaches up and touches the string of pearls around her neck. We're both uncomfortable.

"I'm not the kind of person who talks about such things," she says. "I just couldn't, and no one ever asked."

I press her for details. "Did he ever hurt you?" She lets out little details, one by one. He threw a lamp at her once, then refused to speak to her for three days. Another time, he bought her a new dress, got mad, and proceeded to rip it apart. The last time she was pregnant, seven months along, he threw her across the living room.

Grandma's eyes are blue, the same blue as mine. As I look into those eyes, I think, *Grandma wasn't a battered woman. Impossible.*

Catching my reflection in the glass I say "Grandma, I'm getting a divorce."

"Why?" she asks me. She has stopped rocking.

I look at her and think, *I'm not a battered woman, Grandma.* Yet I manage to say, "He hurt me."

Just before boarding the plane in New York City, I secretly rented a van and moved out of our apartment, while my husband, Jorge, was out of town. It was one week after my twenty-fifth birthday. I had to leave. Over the course of one year, he had broken my front teeth, bruised my arms and legs, and choked me. It's still so hard to say his name, *Jorge.* I understand exactly why Grandma uses "he."

"A lot of women go back," Grandma Ruth says. "They think he'll change."

Grandma knew this fact firsthand. She divorced Grandpa after four children—it was the first divorce in her Catholic family. But then she went back, married him again, and had one more daughter. Five years later, she divorced him for the last time.

"But when you were going out together, he didn't show any signs of violence?" Then she sighs, catching herself. "Oh, they never do, do they?"

No, Grandma, they don't. But we got away. Yes we did.

RACHEL SARAH, TWENTY-SIX, IS PRESENTLY WORKING ON A MEMOIR. SHE LIVES IN NEW YORK CITY AND HAS WRITTEN FOR *MS.* AND *ELLE.*

TO MY GRANDDAUGHTERS

Stephanie Kaplan Cohen

You come from a long line of brave foremothers,
Warrior foremothers,
Who knew without books to tell them they owned their destiny,
Who knew that tears are only useful as soap and water for the soul.

You had a great-great-great-grandmother who knit the stockings for her village
and kept the family fed. She was blind.

One of your great-great-grandmothers saved her family. For two years she
walked around her native Poland, carrying her baby in one arm and small
sewing items in her other arm. She earned passage for herself and two of her

children to come to America. She joyfully reunited with her husband and two older children in a three-room flat in a Brooklyn tenement. Chanah Kaplan never stopped loving life and making fun. At eighty, she took a new husband and swam the waves at Coney Island.

Another of your great-great-grandmothers, Rachelle Dreigerman Schreibman, who seemed so timid, marched with her children and husband across borders in the dead of night. They had no passports and could not bear the thought of their children living through another pogrom. In this country she did quiet battle to educate her children, the youngest of whom, to her joy, earned a college diploma.

Your great-grandmother August Schreibman Kaplan was a slip of a thing, but she too was a warrior, as tall and strong as the mightiest oak. She started out as an errand girl in a factory. In her twenties, she owned her own millinery store. This was in the days before women even had the right to vote. She wanted for her children all the things that would make them secure and accomplished, providing us with dancing lessons, piano lessons, elocution lessons. We wore braces on our teeth and iron arches in our shoes. We learned to type, just in case. In her seventies, she drove to a faraway state, where she made a new and happy life for herself.

I am your grandmother. In my life it has been necessary for me to reach back to our foremothers and remember to be brave, to take chances, to trust and love myself. My life is not done but I would not change a minute of it. I have worked hard, had the joy and pain of raising wonderful children, and the rapture of meeting my grandchildren. I am still amazed and interested by the new discoveries of myself.

I wish for you, beloved granddaughters, joy, health, and the courage to be the most you can be.

STEPHANIE KAPLAN COHEN, SEVENTY-ONE, BEGAN HER WRITING CAREER SEVEN YEARS AGO AFTER RECEIVING A WORD PROCESSOR AS A BAT-MITZVAH GIFT FROM HER HUSBAND. SHE HAS PUBLISHED SHORT STORIES, POETRY, AND ESSAYS IN MANY LITERARY JOURNALS, THE *NEW YORK TIMES,* LOCAL NEWSPAPERS, AND SEVERAL ANTHOLOGIES. HER HUSBAND, THREE CHILDREN, AND SEVEN GRANDCHILDREN ARE A SOURCE OF AMAZEMENT, AMUSEMENT, AND NEVER-ENDING JOY.

DO IT PROPERLY!

Ann Cooper

 f the job's worth doing, it's worth doing properly," my grandmother said when she caught me being lazy or hasty or plain sloppy. The quote still resonates. If I'm tempted to cut corners, or give less than my best to get a job over with, I hear Gran's voice. I'm a middle-aged woman and Gran has been dead for twenty years, yet her legacy lives daily in my got-to-do-it-right attitude.

Gran grew up in Lancashire, England. As a young woman, she worked in the weaving sheds. Folkloric family stories have her wearing wooden-soled clogs and clattering up wet cobbled streets to work the six A.M. shift at the mill. She left her infant son, my father, with a relative and collected him after her long, noisy day at the loom. Later she became a dressmaker, sewing the full-skirted, elaborately-beaded gowns fashionable before World War I changed everything.

Gran filled her house with handmades. When she needed a stair carpet, she wove one. When she wanted a reading lamp, she learned to use a lathe to turn the lamp stem. By the time the lamp was finished, she'd learned wiring and pleated-silk-shade making. When her overstuffed chairs popped springs, she attended night school to learn upholstery. In her "leisure" time, she embroidered, crocheted, made fine lace, and routinely won prizes for her exquisite workwomanship and original designs.

At seventy-five, Gran gave up her home, her woven stair carpet, her crisply upholstered chairs, to look after us when my mother died. "If the job's worth doing . . ."

She did us proud, cooking and counseling, seeing us through our traumatic loss. She never expressed regret at her own disrupted life. She just carried on—housekeeping, dressmaking, gardening, and later great-grandmothering—pragmatic to the end, always doing things right. Her capable hands and strong spirit lasted through ninety-three years of dexterous busyness, pulling garments, gardens, and grandchildren into shape.

I didn't recognize at the time the values she instilled in me. So this is my belated thanks to Gran, for showing me how to set high standards in every task, for modeling "do-it-right," for teaching me there's no venture I can't attempt and that my greatest good is the deed done without fanfare.

ANN COOPER, FIFTY-NINE, AND A GRANDMOTHER TO TWO, IS A PAST "BRIT" AND PRESENT ARDENT COLORADAN. INSPIRED IN PART BY HER GRANDMOTHER'S "DO-IT-RIGHT" EXAMPLE, SHE TOOK UP HER FOURTH CAREER—WRITING—TEN YEARS AGO WHEN HER CHILDREN WERE GROWN. SHE HAS WRITTEN NINE NATURAL HISTORY BOOKS FOR CHILDREN.

SOME WISDOM OVER A CAR RIDE AND CHINESE DINNER

Daniela Uslan

 don't think I'm going to do it before I get married," I said.

"What?"

"I think I'm going to wait . . . you know . . . until I get married . . . to have sex."

"Of course you're not going to wait. Don't be silly." Grandma took her eyes off the road for a moment to look at me in the passenger's seat.

"Why not?" I asked.

Grandma, sporting her usual pink sweatshirt and purple pants, sat forward in the driver's seat and glanced down the road. "Why would you do a thing like that?" she asked.

"What?"

"Why would you wait?"

"Isn't that the right thing to do?" I asked.

"Honey, let me tell you something. What you think is the right thing to do isn't always the real right thing to do."

I glanced at the seat belt hanging next to her, unused. "So does that mean it's wrong to wear my seat belt?"

"No. I don't need to wear it because I'm old. But you do. Because you're young. But that's not what we were talking about. We were talking about sex." She swerved to the side and came into the parking lot of a Chinese restaurant.

While parking the car, she said, "Don't you think Missy has sex?"

"I don't know, I said. Missy is my cousin. She is over twenty years old and lives with her boyfriend, Paul.

"She lives with a man. Doesn't that mean she has sex with him?" Grandma looked over at me, then opened her door and put a leg out.

"I don't know." I was starting to get a little uncomfortable.

"Of course it does. Why else would they live together?"

"Oh." I opened my door and tried to get out of the car.

"I didn't mean you always have to wear a seat belt. Only when the car's moving." She reached over and unbuckled it for me.

"Thanks," I said, embarrassed.

"So think about what I said, okay?" she looked at me expectantly.

"Okay, Grandma," I responded.

"But not now, you're too young now." I was thirteen.

"Yeah. Okay," I said.

"So how did you like that book I gave you?" she asked.

At that point we both got out of the car and walked over to the double doors of the restaurant. "I like it," I said. The book was about a woman who got raped and then later found out the guy who raped her was going to become the president. I told my parents about it the night before. They had been horrified.

Once seated, we looked through the menu carefully. "So, what do you think you're going to have, Daniela?"

"I don't know. I think I'm going on a diet."

"A diet? Why would you go on a diet? You're only thirteen years old!"

"Because this guy I like . . . well . . ." That was the summer I had my first boyfriend. Oddly, knowing a guy liked me confused my life enormously. So much, in fact, that I took the first plane I could to upstate New York so that I wouldn't have to deal with guys for a few weeks.

"Let me tell you something. You should never change yourself for another person. Bad, bad idea." She patted her dyed brown hair than glanced at me again. "Only change for yourself. Listen to the old grandmother on this one. Trust me."

"But I . . . I really like him," I said, staring at the menu in my hands.

"Who cares? Boys come and boys go . . . how old is this boy, anyway?"

"Twelve." I blushed slightly.

"You want to lose weight for a twelve-year-old? He's just out of diapers."

I giggled as the waiter came over. Grandma glanced at me. "Whatever you want," she said.

"Okay . . . I guess I'll have the sesame chicken then."

"Good choice," Grandma commented. "I'll have the chow mein."

When the waiter left, Grandma turned to me again. "So, you're not going on that diet after all?"

"I'll start it tomorrow," I said.

A few weeks later I went home, to my normal life, leaving the heat and humidity of upstate New York behind. I never went on an actual date with my "boyfriend," and I never went on that diet. I tried to think about what I was doing before doing it. Grandma and I never completely agreed on anything . . . except for two ideas. Never change yourself for another person, and what you may think is right isn't necessarily right. But I know that Grandma is always right.

DANIELA USLAN, SIXTEEN, IS A JUNIOR AT DENVER SCHOOL OF THE ARTS. SHE ENJOYS SWING DANCING, READING, WRITING, AND BEING ALIVE. SHE SPENDS MOST OF HER TIME DAYDREAMING AND BEING SILLY. WHEN SHE GROWS UP, SHE WANTS TO BE HAPPY.

ADVENTURER

THE GIVING GIFT

Barbara L. Tylka

nother day, another train station, the same routine. My grandmother and I were traveling in Europe, moving every few days. By the time we returned to the United States, we'd visited Germany, Switzerland, France, and Austria.

The start of our trip had been shaky. As part of my medical-school scholarship, I'd arrived in Europe two months before my grandmother. When I finished studying, she joined me in Germany. I'd taken care of our first two nights' lodging with a student's eye toward economy: a *Gasthaus* in Trier, then an overnight train to Paris.

After our first night together, Grandma good-naturedly informed me that, while she wanted to experience the *real* Europe, meeting underwear-clad men in a narrow stairwell in the middle of the night was a not-to-be-repeated adventure. In the future, our accommodations would have the bathroom attached to the room. After sleeping in her clothes stretched out on a seat on the overnight train to Paris, Grandma added that all future accommodations would be stationary.

Other than those two demands, Grandma left the travel arrangements to me. When we arrived in a new city, she stayed with our luggage, while I changed money and secured a room. In deference to Grandma, I learned to catch a bus or to take the

Bernice Baranowski

streetcars instead of walking everywhere. Though I usually skipped lunch, I remembered this wasn't Grandma's habit and would scout out a café for a midday break.

We enjoyed the formal gardens, hiked in the Black Forest, and picnicked in Switzerland. In the evenings, we'd eat leisurely dinners, then stroll back to our room. We'd read and talk until we were ready to sleep. Grandma shared stories of her youth, of being courted by my grandfather, of her marriage, and of motherhood.

Nonetheless, I worried whether Grandma was enjoying herself. My tight budget didn't allow me to stay in fancy hotels or to dine in four-star restaurants. My pride wouldn't allow Grandma to pay my way. I wondered whether Grandma wished for a different traveling companion, one who could afford to travel in higher style.

I had my answer a few days after we returned home. "Your grandmother can't stop talking about the trip and how you took care of her," my mother told me. "She didn't have to deal with foreign money, or to look for rooms or meals where she didn't understand the language. You made the trip possible for her."

I realized then that I'd discovered more than other cultures and other languages on our European trip. I'd discovered the joy of sharing myself. And in the process, I'd discovered a close new friend, my grandmother.

BARBARA L. TYLKA, THIRTY-EIGHT, WAS IN HER MID-TWENTIES WHEN SHE TRAVELED EUROPE WITH HER GRANDMOTHER. SHE IS CURRENTLY A SURGEON IN PRACTICE IN EASTERN OREGON. IT IS BARBARA'S HOPE THAT, WHEN SHE FINALLY GROWS UP, SHE WILL BE JUST LIKE HER GRANDMOTHER.

MASHIE

Andrea Simon

 have a vivid memory of both my grandmothers visiting me at the same time when I was a child. One was short, gray, and plump—just the way grandmothers were supposed to be. The other—Mashie—was tall and beautiful, wore a mink coat, and called everyone "darling." Even though my other grandmother gave me more money for my birthdays and spent many hours sewing my dresses, I couldn't wait to sneak off to a corner with Mashie, listen to her exotic adventures abroad, and see the jewels she smuggled under her clothing.

Her stories were filled with handsome princes, worldly captains, and cruel villains—and above them all, Mashie reigned supreme. Hers was a world of clear-cut generalities. To her, either you were rich or poor, beautiful or ugly, a good person or a "bastard," faithful or a *kurveh,* a doctor or a "good-for-nothing," a Jew or a *goy.* People were either conspiring to do her in, or couldn't do enough for her.

These labels didn't completely limit Mashie, and she allowed a certain amount of crossover. She readily accepted a *goy* into the family when she found out he was also a doctor, and avoided the potentially explosive issue by always addressing him as "Doctor." One could easily reverse her preconceived notions—a "bastard" could become a *mensch* with a well-chosen compliment, or a "darling" could become a "no-goodnik" by not paying her the proper attention.

Mashie never enjoyed the luxury of finding out who she was. She was too busy

Masha Lew

overcoming upheavals such as early marriage and motherhood, pogroms, epidemics, divorce, death in the family, and religious persecution. Through it all, Mashie learned to survive and retain her dignity. She was up and down, poor and rich, loved and hated—and always colorful and provocative. She was thoroughly her own person—vain, gregarious, suspicious, and egocentric. Although she could be incredibly self-pitying, she was also capable of enormous acts of generosity. She was never dull; her presence seemed to generate the best arguments and the best reconciliations.

Toward the end of her life, Mashie's senility robbed her of any previous duplicity or complicated thoughts. She became docile and childlike, subject to irrational tantrums and bizarre behavior. Her life was reduced to its basic functions, with only increasingly rare lapses into coherence. Perhaps she left life the way she arrived—without memory, with all her inhibitions diminished—a naked, wrinkled, and lonely soul. But there is one major difference. During her journey, she left us her memories to do with them what we will.

Mashie's final irony—and tragedy—is that she had to end her life among the very people she resisted, the old and the sick. If she had had any wits left, she would have cursed God for her helplessness, for her ultimate humiliation.

When I close my eyes, I refuse to see Mashie sitting in a dark room, mumbling incoherently amid the chatter of withered old souls. Instead, I will see Mashie as the mistress of her home, entertaining her guests with amusing gossip and steaming onion rolls. I will nestle under her arm, convinced of her agelessness, convinced that she will be here and the same forever.

ANDREA SIMON, FIFTY-TWO, IS A WRITER AND PHOTOGRAPHER WHO LIVES IN NEW YORK CITY. SHE HAS WORKED AS AN EDITOR, WRITER, AND ENTREPRENEUR FOR MORE THAN TWENTY YEARS. SEVERAL OF HER STORIES AND ARTICLES HAVE BEEN PUBLISHED, AND SHE HAS BEEN A FINALIST IN PRESTIGIOUS COMPETITIONS. HER PHOTOGRAPHY HAS BEEN FEATURED IN GALLERIES AND OTHER VENUES.

HERITAGE OF STRENGTH

Carol L. Goldsmith

he stack of letters sits before me. Each one written in blue ink. The stationery differs. Some is tissue-thin blue air-mail paper, some card stock with *Gumps of San Francisco* stamped discreetly in the corner. The addresses are a pot-pourri of familiar places, family homes, cruise lines, or famous cities. Beside the stack sits a small tidy journal written in the same blue ink and the same familiar hand. It is just one of many. My grandmother left me the gift of stories.

As my daughter was growing up, she loved to crawl into my lap and ask to hear "stories." I didn't have to think very long before I found the threads of

Grandmother's stories weaving themselves together, a blanket of family memories to pass on. My daughter and I have shared many Grandmother stories over the years. Stories from Grandmother's mother coming to California on the Oregon Trail, the story of an eight-year-old in the 1906 San Francisco earthquake, the story about the surprise of giving birth to triplets.

June
Alexander
Hail

The story of Grandmother's wedding and honeymoon in northern Egypt and southern France in the 1920s was a favorite. That adventure lasted a year. At one point, she and my grandfather came across the Mediterranean in an old freighter during a storm. Their Model T in the hold was tossed by the stormy waves and arrived dented and dinged. After landing in Alexandria, they were told the road to the next village was impassable due to mud. Sure that "modern technology" could overcome the local elements, Grandfather and Grandmother took off anyway. A short distance later, they were mired in mud up to their running boards. Several hours passed before a caravan of camels pulled them out. They were towed ignobly back to Alexandria. The camel drivers took everything. Grandmother called it stealing. I wonder if they didn't think of it as payment. She wrote that she felt as though she got the last laugh, however, because "They didn't get our money belts, which were under our clothes."

Later in the trip, she tells of slipping away from the hotel and going into the Valley of the Kings. Climbing up on one of the structures, she sang an aria from *Aida* to Grandfather in the light of the full moon. Her experience singing with the San Francisco Opera Company helped.

It has only been in later years, as I revisited the letters and journals that I found a new message in the stories. A subtle background thread easy to overlook amidst the adventures. Grandmother spoke so often of strength. The strength to maintain one's dignity in the throes of adventure. The strength as one grows older to live fully. Her letters always included reminders of our heritage. She wrote, "You children have such a wonderful heritage of strength, determination, and initiative in your mother and father. May Granddaddy and I squeeze in there too? Just a little?"

CAROL GOLDSMITH IS A VETERAN TEACHER OF TWENTY-FOUR YEARS. SHE GREW UP IN MESA VERDE NATIONAL PARK IN SOUTHWESTERN COLORADO, WHERE SHE WANDERED THE TRAILS, WORKED WITH HER GRANDMOTHER, AND LEARNED TO LOVE STORIES. SHE IS MARRIED AND TEACHES FOURTH GRADE NEAR SAN FRANCISCO. SHE STILL LOVES STORIES.

FAMILY FOOD

Joyce Sidman

ager to create an exciting meal, I open my pantry cupboard to examine its contents. A small jar of olive butter—what was I thinking? Red lentils, which I failed to disguise in spaghetti sauce, an aging bag of risotto with sun-dried tomatoes.

We are not a risotto kind of family. There are four of us, all with different likes and dislikes. The foods we are left with—by process of elimination—are pickles, cheese, bagels, and yogurt.

The same old foods get tedious, though. In desperation, I haul out my grandmother's old recipe box, which I saved when she died. The yellowed cards with her elegant, looping handwriting, plunge me into the past. A proper Bostonian lady, Grandma felt that the basis of all meals was a good cream sauce. My mother tells horror stories of eating Coquilles St. Jacques (creamed scallops) for lunch.

But I remember cookies—Grandma cookies. Hopeful, I dive into the recipe box.

Predictably, there are stacks of recipes for custards and creams, and sauces with enough butterfat to kill an army. The filing system is totally disorganized. If there is a method, I can't find it. Lamb Marinade follows Pecan Pie, which is also grouped with Bernaise Sauce. There are at least three index tabs marked *C* (Cakes, Cookies, and Chicken??). Under one of the *M*'s, I find a recipe for croissants—in French. *"Proceder comme pour la brioche…,"* it begins.

This is Grandma, all right: strong-willed, creative, and scatterbrained. She painted beautifully, spoke three languages, and sang like an angel. But she lost her reading glasses so often that we children vowed to invent a glasses-finding device. I was often compared to her as a child. This was not usually a compliment, but I accepted it proudly as the badge of an *artiste*.

Grandma was not only creative, she admired spunk—in her own proper, old-fashioned way. Even when she grew quite deaf, she loved to meet new people and try new things. And sure enough, there in the recipe box, I found some recipes that were pretty radical for her: Eggplant Provençale, Jamaican Banana Fritters, and Santa Fe Three-Bean Rarebit.

I also find, in my own childish scrawl, a recipe for Goody Bars.

Goody Bars! I still make them, much to the delight of my family.

In fact, the biggest surprise of this whole recipe box is how familiar it all is. The zucchini bread, the turkey casserole, the blueberry pie, the bulging section of cookies and bread, the ten different recipes for bran muffins. This woman cooked just like I do: worried about dinner, but dreaming of dessert. Here I am, thinking I'm forging my way through mealtime on my own, when I am really standing shoulder to shoulder with my grandmother.

I'm sure Grandma didn't keep the same four staples in her refrigerator as we do. In fact, I don't think she'd even heard of bagels when she died. I know she liked yogurt, though, and was partial to cheddar cheese. In fact, her daily diet was probably just as boring as mine.

And yet, she had once tried Three-Bean Rarebit.

With new heart, I approach the cupboard. Perhaps tonight is the night for risotto. I might even throw in some mushrooms with those sun-dried tomatoes. The lentils I'll feed to the birds, but there might be hope yet for the olive butter. Smeared on bran muffins, maybe? No, I know my limits.

I also know if I make Goody Bars for dessert, anything—including the risotto— will be forgiven. Grandma taught me well.

JOYCE SIDMAN IS A REGULAR COLUMNIST FOR THE *ST. PAUL PIONEER PRESS*. HER ESSAYS, POETRY, AND FICTION HAVE APPEARED IN NUMEROUS PUBLICATIONS, SUCH AS *YANKEE, THE CHRISTIAN SCIENCE MONITOR,* AND *CRICKET* MAGAZINE.

Doris Prowse Robinson

Margaret Gepner

CITY GIRL

дia

ana loved the wind. She was a fresh-air fiend just like her mother. Nana turned her face to the wind like she was smelling flowers, while my mother always liked everything closed up tight with the drapes pulled. As a child, I spent most of my weekends with Nana, resting in the familiar hub of the urban wilderness of the Windy City.

My nose always leads the sense parade back to those times. The familiar odor of bus exhaust warmed me as people rushed by, a marching surge toward populating all those skyscrapers, like so many ants loose and purposeful in their shiny kingdom. I loved sitting next to Nana on the bus, watching the busy streets pass by. She always knew just where to get off the bus. When I marveled at this, she just shrugged and said, "I'm just a city girl, you know."

The El-train was a whole other living current of activity, running like exposed veins above the dense stop-and-go of the streets. We rode the El and tangled our way through the loop of downtown. I crossed my legs like the women in their commuter skirts, folding my hands over a shopping bag as if it was my pocketbook. Getting off the train on State Street, we'd slip through the spinning doors into Marshall Fields, where Nana would buy a box of those heavenly Frango mint chocolates. I swear I could taste those mints while holding the box wrapped in plastic.

Two doors down from Nana's building was a Laundromat. The hot linty blast pricked my nostrils with a welcome cloud as we passed by. The smell of the old elevator in Nana's building and the cold feel of the heavy iron gate filled me with cozy anticipation of making Toll House cookies in her tiny kitchen. I later watched *I Love Lucy* and *The Dick Van Dyke Show* while she hemmed a skirt or read a book.

Nana was always reading a book. At night she'd read me stories and for those scary deep-in-the-forest scenes, she'd chime in with the hiss of the steam heater as I pulled up the covers. Soon the hiss became the tender whispering of the prince. I went to bed listening to the lull of horns and sirens and Nana's steady breathing. Through the thin shades, the city streets below offered a soothing night-light. I could always find my way to the bathroom. I never had to be afraid of the dark, since I never really experienced total darkness those nights in Nana's apartment.

The darkness came when Nana died one day in late September. I wore a snug navy-blue pants suit to the funeral and couldn't look at anybody. Then the wind that Nana had so loved kicked up. From my powdered nose right down to my painted toes I stood up tall, like the city girl I was and always would be.

IN THIRTY-FIVE YEARS, DIA HAS RESIDED IN EIGHT STATES, TEN DIFFERENT CITIES, AND ABOUT TWENTY-FIVE HOUSES. "HOME" IS SIMPLY THE PLACE WHERE SHE FINDS HERSELF. DIA CURRENTLY LIVES IN ASHLAND, OREGON, AND SPENDS A LOT OF TIME UP ON MT. SHASTA IN NORTHERN CALIFORNIA. SHE LOVES SPICY BLUE CORN CHIPS, SONGS BY GREG BROWN, AND SLEEPING UNDER THE STARS.

SWIMMING LESSONS

Jeaninne M. Escallier Kato

arjorie Elizabeth Willets is the part of me that paddles upstream when it would be easier to turn my boat around. My mother says we are a lot alike—stubborn, strong-willed, and embedded in our beliefs. When Grandma Willets and I are in a room together, there is a palpable wall of strength.

In her early fifties, Grandma Willets stepped in to run our household when my mother was recuperating from a devastating divorce. There was no time for sentiment when meals had to be cooked and clothes had to be washed. God probably coined the phrase, "Cleanliness is next to Godliness," when He made my Grandmother Willets. I didn't dare sneak that occasional cigarette in the backyard or come in one minute late from a date when my

Grandma Willets was around. She made that perfectly clear. *No, sir . . . ree . . . bub.*

Her passion for traveling ran a close second to her passion for cleanliness and order. Car trips with Grandma Willets, from Death Valley to San Francisco, dotted the landscape of my childhood. While my brother, my cousin, and I played silly games in the backseat, Grandma Willets drove steadily and cautiously, like a captain at sea. She would often interrupt our playtimes with factual bits of information related to the terrain of the moment.

One of those car trips binds us forever. On a hot summer afternoon in the middle of the Sequoia National Forest, I just had to go for a swim. Being thirteen, impulsive, and always ready for adventure, I talked Grandma Willets into stopping the car. With wild abandon, I dove into the icy river; minutes later, I was being swept away, unable to catch my breath. I was forced to swim to a sandbar that separated me from Grandma and the rest of my family. "Grandma," I screamed, "I can't swim back!" Grandma Willets ran frantically to a tree that had fallen across the creek and yelled back, "Swim to this log and I will hoist you up." *Okay, Grandma,* I thought, *I won't let you down.* I swam to the log and into her grasp.

Grandma Willets still has nightmares about that day. She always says, "All I could think about was having to tell your mother that you had drowned." And I always say, "Oh, Grandma, I knew I was going to be fine."

I completely trusted my grandmother to handle that situation and take care of me. Because of Marjorie Elizabeth Willets, I have learned to have that same belief and trust in myself.

JEANINNE ESCALLIER KATO IS A FORTY-THREE-YEAR-OLD "TEENAGER" WHO HAS BEEN A TEACHER FOR TWENTY YEARS. SHE IS A PUBLISHED WRITER AND THE RECENT RECIPIENT OF "TEACHER OF THE YEAR" FOR THE CALIFORNIA CONTINUATION EDUCATION ASSOCIATION, DISTRICT 12. SHE RESIDES IN ROCKLIN, CALIFORNIA, WITH HER HUSBAND, GLENN, HER FOSTER CHILD, ERIC, AND HER CANINE AND FELINE "CHILDREN."

SAFE
HARBOR

For Granny Christine

TAKING CARE
Crystal E. Wilkinson

ou nurtured me, embraced me in warm, soft hugs. You were not the one who gave me birth, but I was your sugar baby. It was you who blew dust from my eyes, nursed my fevers, kissed my bruises, and encouraged my dreams.

You were married at fourteen, cleaned houses for white folks and still managed to raise seven children, plus me, and attended Granddaddy's every need. You were always somebody's something. I never really remember you taking care of yourself.

Maybe that's why you insisted that I *take care* every time we parted. Maybe that is why you pulled me close and whispered "Girl, if you don't take care of *you*, ain't gonna be nobody to do it." You told me to learn to take care of *me*. You said every woman should.

Whenever life got too hard, it was to you I ran. You always insisted that I put my feet up. You would cook biscuits and blackberries or whatever I wanted. You would tell me not to worry about the kids, to just rest. Only with you could I stop being the strong black woman and just be. You would look into the tiredness in my eyes, beyond the throbbing headache, and tell me that I wouldn't be any good to anybody dead. That *taking care* was essential.

When you died, I didn't know what to do. Even when I thought I was coping, I would catch myself all clenched up tight as a fist, blood pressure rising, head hurting, suffering from superwoman blues. I was always working two jobs, taking care of three children alone, being the lean-on-me for all my friends.

Not shedding a tear toward nobody for nothing. I wanted and needed you. I thought your arms were my only solace.

You have been gone for some time and still, "Girl, you got to take care of yourself," echoes like thunder at those precise moments when I have had enough.

I am on the edge of understanding, on the edge of *taking care*, like you said. I am slowly learning, growing toward balance.

Now, when I run, it is to my house, where I plan these long, leisurely dates with my strong-sister self. I get a baby-sitter for the weekend. I fix my favorite foods. Eat. Turn off the phone and light some scented candles or incense. I sink into a tub of hot bubbles with a good book. Sometimes when my burden is heavy and Billie Holiday hits that lonesome note, I cry. I wrap my arms around my own body in praise of your memory and myself.

CRYSTAL E. WILKINSON, THIRTY-FIVE, A POET AND SHORT FICTION WRITER, GREW UP IN INDIAN CREEK, KENTUCKY. SHE IS A FOUNDING MEMBER OF THE AFFRILACHIAN POETS AND THE BLUEGRASS BLACK ARTS CONSORTIUM. CRYSTAL IS THE MOTHER OF GERALD, ELAINIA, AND DELANIA.

Edna Michael

Christine Wilkinson

MAGA

Ann E. Michael

 lie in bed in a cool room. The sun has only recently set; fireflies are low in the grass. I can see them blinking in the clover because this room is below grade: Its one window is curiously high on the wall and its view is mostly grass.

My little sister is asleep beside me. It's humid, and overly warm; our cotton sheet clings to us. I hear muffled voices of grown-ups. My father and great-uncle are chatting on the back patio. I know their backs are to the house. They are facing the river, not each other. They have their hands in their pockets. My mother and grandmother are moving around in the kitchen. I hear the dishes clatter, the pipes shudder when the tap is turned on. I hear their voices, but I can't tell what it is they are saying. Except every once in a while my grandmother's voice rises and falls clearly, saying, "Oh, well!"

I am very young, perhaps seven. I never get to sleep easily. I lie awake, mulling over the day's events, planning for tomorrow. I build forts and castles and tepees in my mind. I imagine running faster than any of my cousins, and being able to fly. I catch a huge fish from the Eel River, and I remember stories my great-grandmother told me about settlers who lived in log cabins here and whose neighbors were Indians. I meet an Indian in my mind. The Indian is kind. I give him milk and biscuits, and he gives me pretty feathers and a bone necklace. I realize all those people from long ago are dead now. I think about being dead, and the room seems darker and more smothering. I know I should sleep, but I want to cry out for comfort.

I hear my grandmother's light step outside the door. She's a small lady, her tread is exceedingly soft, but somehow I can always hear her approach, as though I am especially wired for it. I venture an illicit, loud whisper: "Maga?"

A stripe of light widens on the opposite wall, and I see her face peering in from the door. "Oh, why aren't you asleep!" she scolds tenderly.

"I can't sleep, Maga. I'm scared."

She steps into the room, closing the door gently, and stands by the bed. She runs her dry, warm fingers over my hot, damp face. Her hand feels cooler than the air; it tickles a little, but soothingly. I always tell my parents about what scares me: that I'm afraid to die, that I hate the idea of losing all the beautiful, interesting things of earth and missing the people I love so my heart could break. But I don't talk about it to my grandmother. I just let her soothe me as though I were two instead of seven. I just lie quietly in her spare bed and breathe the moist and somewhat musty air, listening to my sister's steady breathing and the sounds of grown-ups murmuring. I close my eyes, and I know the lightning bugs are flashing a little higher off the ground. I know that in the intense stillness of this hot night, the corn is growing taller and the river is slowly moving under the bridge, right through town and out past the fields, moving like my grandmother's fingers move across my skin, and I am asleep.

A hickory leaf floats slowly down the Eel River, under the arches of the bridge where I have tried to lure summer days into capture. I dream of mosquitoes, daylilies, fields of corn. I dream the scent of lavender water and pink soap. I remember Maga, and memory becomes a darning egg or a wooden spool: something small, tactile, hidden in a basket or a candle box, along with pictures of relatives I can't name and now-elderly people in their sepia-tinted youths. Memory is a wrinkled hand soft upon the brow of a sleepless child, and when I try to grasp it, it evaporates at once. It teaches me about letting go as well as about returning.

ANN E. MICHAEL IS A 1998 RECIPIENT OF A TEN-THOUSAND-DOLLAR PENNSYLVANIA COUNCIL ON THE ARTS POETRY FELLOWSHIP. HER POETRY HAS BEEN PUBLISHED IN *THEMA, ICARUS, MINIMUS,* AND OTHER LITERARY JOURNALS. SHE IS THE MOTHER OF A SEVEN-YEAR-OLD DAUGHTER AND AN EIGHT-YEAR-OLD SON AND RESIDES IN COOPERSBURG, PENNSYLVANIA.

LUNCH FOR A PRINCESS

Yvette Stack

The spring that I was nine, Grandma Carrier came to visit us for ten days. Each year, after Easter, Grandma took the train from Winnipeg to Edmonton and arrived decked out in a new suit with matching accessories.

What made this year different, however, was that her identical twin, Juliette, came with her. Aunt Juliette and Grandma both liked to "dress smartly" as they put it. So this time two elegant ladies descended gracefully from the first-class sleeping car of the CN Supercontinental. They both looked smashing, and they knew it!

What I loved best about Grandma's visits was that I could come home from school for lunch and we would have time alone together. Because my mother taught school and my sisters were all in high school, I usually took lunch to school or came home to an empty house, made myself a sandwich, and watched *The Flintstones*.

Grandma reveled in preparing me elegant lunches. A steaming bowl of homemade soup and a sandwich, cut into four triangles with the crusts trimmed off, awaited me when I entered the kitchen. For a special treat, she made a unique creation called "egg in a hole." She buttered a thick slice of bread on both sides, cut out the center, broke an egg into the hole and fried the concoction on both sides.

This particular year, two heads peered out the kitchen window, watching my approach. Two pairs of hands served me lunch on my mother's best china and patted my head. This year there was also dessert. Aunt Juliette made her famous lemon tarts with decadent shortbread pastry and topped with whipped cream. These were accompanied by tea, hot and strong, with canned milk and two teaspoons of sugar.

After lunch, we watched *General Hospital*. Grandma would brush my hair and tell me I looked like a princess. After being kissed and hugged and warned to "be careful," I returned to school. I never told my sisters or my parents about the royal treatment I received every noon hour, and neither did Grandma or Auntie. There was a tacit agreement that this was our secret, and there was no need for anyone else to know about it.

Eight months after that visit, Grandma died suddenly, followed less than a year later by Aunt Juliette. Twenty-five years have passed since then, but even now, when I see little girls walking home from school at noon, I think of that special time in my childhood, and I hope that they too, are going home to someone who loves them.

YVETTE STACK, SIXTY, IS A RETIRED ELEMENTARY-SCHOOL TEACHER. SHE TEACHES MUSIC EDUCATION PART TIME AT THE UNIVERSITY OF ALBERTA AND IS A CHURCH ORGANIST. SHE HAS SIX ADULT DAUGHTERS. SHE LOVES TO READ, CROSS-COUNTRY SKI, AND HIKE IN THE BEAUTIFUL ROCKY MOUNTAINS. SHE ALSO LOVES TO TRAVEL AND SPENT THREE MONTHS HIKING AND EATING HER WAY THROUGH SPAIN LAST FALL.

HOLIDAY

Jennifer Fisher Bryant

Many voices mingle in memory.
Toweled hands swipe spoon-licked
casseroles;
steam clouds rise from blackberry pies
like smoke signals, warning off any man
who enters this enclave of feminine
tradition.

My two small hands polish pots and pans
as I listen to the chatter of women.
In Grandmother's winter kitchen
there were always too many cooks—
but the soup was the richest in town.

JENNIFER FISHER BRYANT, THIRTY-EIGHT, IS THE AUTHOR OF FOURTEEN NON-
FICTION BOOKS, INCLUDING *THOMAS MERTON: POET, PROPHET, PRIEST* (EERDMANS,
1997). HER POEM "BRICKS" WON THE 1997 MANAYUNK (PA) POETRY CONTEST. SHE
LIVES IN CHESTER COUNTY WHERE SHE CONDUCTS WRITING WORKSHOPS FOR THE
PENNSYLVANIA COUNCIL ON THE ARTS.

IN MY GRANDMOTHER'S KITCHEN

Stephanie Davison

ight washes over my shoulder from the open front door and the kitchen window. So bright is this summer sun that it bounces off the brown refrigerator and back into my eyes. She is standing over me and demonstrating how to roll out sugar-cookie dough. I am five years old. My towheaded blond locks are drafted in Dutch-boy style to match her own. With my knees tucked under and my heels propping up my bottom, I am happily seated upon the vinyl swivel stool at the cutting board in my Grandmother's kitchen. Grasping the counter, I twirl myself from side to side impatiently.

She wears burgundy polyester pants and a pink-and-white print top of a light cotton blend, short sleeved, buttoned up the front, and lightly pressed. It is untucked like a tunic. There is an unevenness in the way her blouse falls, one side filled with her large and sagging breast, the other flat and hollow. Her blouse rests unevenly upon a roll of fat about her waist, and again upon her hips. She brushes her gray, soft hair away from her wide forehead with a floured hand. To me, she is perfect.

Her blue eyes look easy and deep, with a Nordic blue that has not since been matched in my memory, icy and warm at the same time, lovely and patient.

There has never been another who was mine so completely as my grandmother, my sanctuary. And in that kitchen bathed in sunlight, the two of us together spent countless hours forming cookie dough, while she shaped my ideas of what it was to love and be loved.

STEPHANIE DAVISON, THIRTY-FOUR, IS A NORTHWEST COAST WRITER WHO USES THE NATURAL ENVIRONMENT FOR MANY OF THE IMAGES SHE CREATES IN HER POETRY, SHORT STORIES, AND CHILDREN'S BOOKS.

Hilda Helena Hanson

MY RESCUER

Monique Avakian

My sister and I were rescued by our grandmother, who took us in and loved us after our abusive, heroin-addicted, teenage mother ran away and left us all for good.

My grandmother lived a life filled with difficulties and obstacles that she could not find her way around. The biggest impediment was a lack of education, a decision forced upon her at age fourteen.

One day my great-grandfather stormed home and announced that the four girls would have to quit school immediately and go to work so that the two boys in the family could finish high school. His word became law as he chopped off the girls' braids and sent them to bed hungry and crying. The next day, the sisters searched for work as maids.

The weight of that decision hurt my grandmother deeply. She was an extremely intelligent and philosophical person, and she loved going to school. She had a glorious mind, but ended up working as a menial laborer all of her life, inside and outside of the home.

She raised one daughter who was a difficult child from the beginning. After years of struggling, just when it seemed as though my mother would actually pull herself together and allow my grandmother to move on with her own life, there came another sudden decision. My grandmother awoke one fateful morning to a rudely written note, an empty bedroom closet, and two small sleeping children to care for—one handicapped and one completely out of control.

I would not be alive today were it not for my grandmother's sacrifice. I never could have cared for my own daughter properly without my grandmother as a positive model. She was a strong, intelligent, poor, uneducated woman, tied to the kitchen, unknown, unsung, but never, ever, forgotten by me for her courage, love, and tenderness to all.

She's been gone now from this world for eleven years. But she does send a sign now and again, to let me know she's still rooting for me.

MONIQUE AVAKIAN, THIRTY-SIX, IS A POET, MOTHER, PEACE ACTIVIST, AND FREELANCE WRITER. SHE LIVES IN HASTINGS-ON-HUDSON, NEW YORK, AND TRIES TO DIG IN THE DIRT OUTSIDE AS MUCH AS POSSIBLE.

BEADS OF
REMEMBRANCE

Mexie M. Cottle

 close my eyes and memories of her fill my mind. She was a tiny woman, only about four feet ten inches, but she stood tall in the minds and hearts of my brother and me. She wore her snow-white hair in a little bun at the back of her head, and she had blue eyes. She wore her dresses ankle length as long as she lived and loved necklaces, which she called "beads." I have one of her necklaces, made of some kind of wood, very dark. When I wear it, I find myself touching it a lot, and each bead brings a memory.

I hear her gentle voice, telling me stories or reading to my brother and me from the Bible.

She taught me lessons my mother didn't have time to teach: tolerance, humility, good morals, and as much patience as I could absorb.

Her room was my refuge when trouble threatened. She was never too busy to listen to me chatter and never, ever, laughed at my flights of fancy as the rest of the family did. She took me for walks and to the general store, and in the spring we picked greens. She would teach me which wild plant was good for greens and which plants made good medicine.

Grandma hand sewed a rag doll for me. I named the doll Dorothy Ann and loved her dearly. My grandmother also knit mittens for my brother and me, the four needles flashing in her small hands while she told me stories.

I am now seventy-one years old, but to this day, if I am angry with someone and feel a desire to get even, I will hear her soft voice saying, " Vengeance is mine, saith the Lord," and I cool off.

I felt a part of me was missing when she died. She was the person I most wanted to be like for my own grandchildren when they came along.

MEXIE M. COTTLE GREW UP IN THE MOUNTAINS, DAUGHTER OF A MINISTER, AND THE YOUNGEST OF A LARGE FAMILY. SHE HAS BEEN MARRIED FOR FIFTY-THREE YEARS AND HAS FOUR CHILDREN AND NINE GRANDCHILDREN. SHE IS RETIRED FROM THE UNIVERSITY OF KENTUCKY AND HAS BEEN WRITING FOR EIGHT YEARS.

LOVE NICKELS

H.E.R. Ward

 think of Nana when it rains. She would feel sorry for my brother and me because we couldn't go outside to play. She would send me to the store for apples. I would have to cut the apples, while receiving a lesson on how to cut them so I didn't "waste half the apple." After the apples were cut, Nana would make an apple dumpling. I experienced a warm feeling as I walked through the house smelling the apples and cinnamon and nutmeg. We were allowed to steal a taste from the pot as often as we wished. It was the only time anyone was allowed to go into Nana's pots.

Every Saturday, Nana would make bread. There would be dough rising all over the house, covered with damp towels. Every Sunday morning, Nana would be up before all of us and she would make some of the dough as rolls and some as fried bread. The fried bread was my favorite. Before Sunday school, Nana would fry the bread in an old iron skillet. Sometimes she would let us flip the dough. To eat that bread with melted butter trickling down my chin was such fun! After Sunday school the whole family would have the hot rolls with fried apples and bacon.

When I was a little, little girl, it was my job to scratch Nana's scalp before she washed her hair on Saturday night so it would be fresh for Sunday. I got a dime for this job. Boy, did I hate what I had to do to get that dime! Nana would sit on a pillow on the floor and I would sit on a chair with my legs dangling on each side of her. I had to make small parts so I would get all of her scalp. That seemed to take too long for me, so I would try to make bigger parts. I couldn't understand how Nana knew that I was trying to get finished faster. That was one of the great mysteries of my "little hilda" days. I wish I could earn that dime today.

Monday was wash day. Nana took pride in her laundry. She washed our clothes and also took in laundry. The bluing was mixed to dip the white clothes in so they would be sparkling white. The Linit starch was boiled on the stove so everything would be stiff and firm. She had an old washer with a wringer, which she hooked up to the sink. Standing barefoot, she pulled out the white, bright, stainless clothes, and then hung them out on the clothesline, which ran from our back window to a pole at the end of the yard.

On Tuesdays, Nana set up the ironing board by the kitchen table and ironed, again barefoot, for hours. Each piece was folded with love and care and placed in neat piles on the kitchen table so that they looked professionally laundered. Nana ironed everything from sheets to pajamas. She taught me to iron on the underwear and handkerchiefs.

My dresses were always starched and beautifully ironed. When I came home from school for lunch, Nana would braid my hair again and put on hair ribbons that matched the new starched dress I would wear back to school. The next morning, I wore the previous afternoon's dress, ironed again. I never wore the same dress all day.

Nana was my comforter. She was my warm hugs, not with arms, but with love nickels. She would slip a nickel in the palm of my hand and close my fingers around it without a word. It was supposed to be our secret.

Nana was "my mother" because my mother had to go out and earn a living. She was there when I got home from school. She came to school when a teacher sent for a parent. She took me downtown to pay bills, which was our special fun excursion that always ended with a thirty-five-cent banana split. She was the one who made me see that I had to be able to deal with the harsh facts of life because I was "a colored girl" and life would be hard for me. She felt so much pride in what I accomplished.

She was a quiet soul but was always there with her strength for me to lean on. Nana and all my ancestors are still with me. I have called on Nana to help me in pain and anguish and disappointment. She has found a way to let me know she was there and that what I was doing was OK, that I would be OK. When I meditate, my ancestors always come to me, and she is the one that leads them.

Nana has always been there for me, from birth to my mature years. Her warmth covers me with soothing, comforting strength that makes me know that I can do whatever I set out to do. She is the foundation that keeps me standing firm upon the soil to reach up to touch all there is for me to experience.

HILDA E. WARD, SIXTY-SIX, IS A MOTHER OF THREE, GRANDMOTHER OF FOUR, AND A GREAT-GRANDMOTHER. SHE WAS A NURSE FOR MANY YEARS, A HEALTH EDUCATOR IN A LONG ISLAND HIGH SCHOOL FOR TWENTY-FOUR YEARS, AND HAS TAUGHT IN COLLEGE. SHE RETIRED SEVERAL YEARS AGO BUT NOW FINDS HERSELF WORKING AS A PEER HEALTH EDUCATION COORDINATOR AT THE UNIVERSITY OF VIRGINIA.

Anna Gumes

Frances Dovi

MEETING ON THE PATH

Carol Dovi

I sat in a circle among a handful of participants at a workshop. The topic of that workshop eludes me, as ten years have passed. The opening exercise of the workshop stays with me still.

After introductions, the facilitator led the group in a guided visualization. "Close your eyes," her soothing voice instructed, "and imagine walking along a path through the woods. Someone is coming to meet you on the path, and this person has a gift for you."

My grandmother greeted me on that path. It seemed natural to see her stocky five-foot-one frame approaching me, even though she had been dead for five years. I smiled as I noticed she wore her "uniform"—navy-blue housedress, black kneesocks, and her favorite black Daniel Green slippers. We exchanged no words when we met on the path but embraced each other.

Tears flowed in the safety of that embrace. The encounter brought with it the full realization of how this woman's constant and unconditional love had affected me. So much of my young life seemed about performance—grades in school, accomplishments in extracurricular activities, standings in the popularity ratings among my peers. In my mind, I never measured up. I felt insecure, unhappy with myself, and deeply depressed, sometimes entertaining thoughts of suicide

My "performance" never mattered to my grandmother. I was Carol Anna, her granddaughter, and that was enough. She never shared words of wisdom, or even said, "I love you," but her eyes, smile, and attention spoke volumes. Re-experiencing her unconditional acceptance in that exercise of imagination, I realized how critical that love had been in my own difficult journey toward self-acceptance.

Frances Dovi never had time to do the introspective work that I spent time doing. She left Sicily and sailed to America with her six-year-old son, my father, after her husband, Giovanni, finally saved enough money to send for her. She worked full-time at a clothing factory, hand-sewing buttonholes in suits. She ran an apartment building that she and my grandfather owned on Somerset Street in New Brunswick, New Jersey. She cared for her bedridden husband for ten years following his stroke. And she adored me and all her grandchildren.

We played under her heavy Mediterranean dining-room table when we visited. We sat at that same table and followed Nanny's command to *"mangia,"* "eat," as she served us pasta with spareribs and meatballs. She recounted for us what people had won on the game shows she watched that day. Having experienced a life filled with hard work and of nothing handed to her, she was amazed that contestants won such wonderful prizes on those game shows. "You be sooprised," she'd say as enthusiastically as if she had won. "This nicea boy, he won a new car! Godda bless."

Although nothing was handed to Nanny, she always gave. She financed the educa-

123

tion of family members in her small Sicilian hometown and provided a place for relatives to stay when they came to work in the United States. In my grandfather's hospital room after his stroke, I witnessed Nanny lovingly feed her recently robust husband slices of peach and then turn and offer some of the fruit to the grateful stranger in the next bed.

After a visit to my grandmother's house, she pressed a twenty-dollar bill into each grandchild's hand. This was the same woman, who on a shopping trip to replace her well-worn apron, refused to buy the apron because she thought it was too expensive. "Sonoma beech, I'ma no pay seven dollars for an apron," she said, and left the store.

Since my experience of my grandmother's presence in that workshop ten years ago, I feel her with me every day. I'm especially aware of her presence when I provide someone with nourishment, whether in the form of a meal or the offering of support and encouragement. At these times, I almost hear her voice saying, "Godda bless."

CAROL DOVI, FORTY-TWO, WORKS AS AN ADMISSIONS REPRESENTATIVE FOR A PROPRIETARY SCHOOL. SHE ASPIRES TO LIVE HER LIFE WITH THE SAME DEPTH OF LOVE AND COURAGE EXHIBITED BY HER GRANDMOTHER, FRANCES DOVI.

A QUILT LIKE A PAINTING

Roberta Hartling Gates

he moon sheds soft watery light on Grandma's quilt. It is so lovely: pale green and white with roses embroidered in pink. Lying beneath it, I feel special, the oldest and best of all her grandchildren. In the rest of my life, it is different, though. At school, in my third-grade class, I am one of the misfits, so shy I hide behind trees during recess. At home, my mother yells at me, my father ignores me. He sits in his chair, smoking cigarettes and waiting for us to grow up. My mother scurries to please him, trying to make him respond.

But here, at Grandma's house, there is no husband, no father. Grandma is queen, and she does what she wants. During the day, she lugs rocks, hurls corn at her geese, wrestles with big balls of dough. She wears a housedress and apron with thick cotton stockings. The bun at the back of her head is coiled tight as a snake. But at night, she is transformed: I see her drifting to bed in a long white gown, her breasts saggy and low, her long gray hair springing away from her head, all witchy and wild.

But I am intrigued: Witches have power, others do what they say. My bachelor uncles, for instance, fall all over themselves to do things for Ma. She tells them to mow hay, to combine oats, to plant this field or that one, and they do it, no questions asked. They love her, but they fear her too. My mother is even more that way. Whenever Grandma comes over, I see her shrinking away, sliding into herself. I see it, but I don't understand why.

I finger the quilt, the embroidered names of all the farm ladies who worked on it. Each year the Royal Neighbors Club makes a quilt for one of its members, and when they are finished they sign it, like a painting in a museum. I like to think about Grandma's friends, all of them royal, bending over their needles, stitching away for a solid year to make her this quilt. That is how special she is to them. I wish my mother had a quilt like this one, or a club to belong to. Maybe then she could stop scurrying.

Outside the branches move, scattering moonlight over the roses. I scrunch down deeper, and the quilt settles around me. Although only eight years old, I know that someday I will have breasts and a wild head of hair. No one will yell at me, and I'll be special, the way Grandma says. Her quilt will be mine, and I'll sleep under it always.

ROBERTA HARTLING GATES, FIFTY-TWO, RECEIVED HER M.F.A. IN FICTION WRITING FROM VERMONT COLLEGE IN 1995. PREVIOUS WORK HAS APPEARED IN *THE LOUISVILLE REVIEW, PASSAGER,* AND THE *AMERICAN ANTHOLOGY OF MIDWESTERN POETRY.* SHE TEACHES HIGH-SCHOOL ENGLISH AT AN ISLAMIC SCHOOL FOR GIRLS AND LIVES IN RIVERSIDE, ILLINOIS, WITH HER HUSBAND AND TWO SONS.

MY BEST FRIEND

Paula Hagar

he youngest of ten children, Gram lived her entire life in the family house where all ten kids were born. She lived with her oldest sister, my great-aunt Nell, whom we called "Nana." Nana did all the cooking and housecleaning, while Grandma worked and paid the bills.

Gram worked her entire life as a secretary. I loved to go meet her after school at her office. I'd roll the creamy white bond paper into the heavy old metal Underwood typewriter and try to create words fresh from my mind on that thick linen paper.

Grandma was my very best friend when I was a kid. She let me do anything I wanted, never raised her voice to me, and loved me more, I thought, than my own mother. Now that I'm an adult I know why. Mom didn't really want me to be born a mere nine months and six days after her wedding day. She wasn't ready for me to arrive and need a mother. "Your resentment toward that child is showing." That's what Gram said to my mom, weeks after my birth. Perhaps it was at that point that I became Grandma's pet.

She was delighted to relieve Mom of me, and every Saturday we'd go shopping together out to the Seaway Shopping Center, and she'd buy me lunch at the J. J. Newberry's lunch counter. We'd spend each Saturday night watching Lawrence Welk blow his bubbles out into the orchestrated air, and watch the couples dancing around and around, knowing someday I'd find a Prince Charming who'd sweep me off the dance floor into the night full of bubbles. We played dozens of kinds of double solitaire far into the night, and then I'd struggle wearily upstairs and lay in the bed my own mother had grown up lying awake in, wondering why *her* parents loved her brother more than her.

When I turned twelve and had to go to junior high, I could no longer pretend I didn't live in the real world—or with Gram. It was about that time that I began to pull away from her, and no longer wanted to spend Saturday nights at her house. I wanted to be with my own girlfriends on Saturday night, roaming the streets like packs of she-wolves in heat. I didn't want to be with an old grandmother playing cards to the tunes of Lawrence Welk when the other kids were out boy teasing.

And so I saw her less and less, and when they finally diagnosed her with colon cancer the following year, it was way too late. When Mom put her in the nursing home in the final months, I couldn't bring myself to go see her. Except once, and she lay there in that tiny bed like a skeleton with a bit of skin holding her bones together—lay there and looked at me and then turned her back to me. I just stood there, crushed, and then left. It wasn't until years later that I realized she was not doing it to be cruel. She didn't want me to see her like that. I didn't see her again like that until she was in her casket. I broke down at the funeral parlor and did not stop crying for a week. I'd wake up in the middle of the night screaming because all I could smell were flowers, flowers, and more flowers. And I miss her so very, very much, but I know she knows how much I loved her, and love her still. She visits me often in my dreams, and I awake happy, knowing I've spent some time with her.

She was not like most grandmothers I hear about. She never cooked a single meal I can remember. She didn't teach me to knit, crochet, sew, or embroider. She was not the spewer of great words of sagelike wisdom. They tell me she was the classic crazy old-lady driver who was all over the road. I only remember tooling down the streets in her old gray Rambler, both of us excited to be headed out to the Seaway Shopping Center. They tell me she was one of the most bigoted women alive, but I never saw that side of her. I never heard her yell the way my mom says she did. She was my very best friend. She gave me the first unconditional love I ever had, and without her in my childhood, I'd not have known love.

PAULA HAGAR, FORTY-THREE, IS A WRITER, POET, AND PHOTOGRAPHER BY DAY, AND A COMPUTER LEGAL ASSISTANT BY NIGHT, WHO LIVES IN DENVER, COLORADO. SHE MISSES HER GRANDMOTHER DAILY AND WRITES OFTEN OF HER CHILDHOOD IN HER VIGNETTES.

THE CAMEO

Janet I. Buck

I was born with bones like broken pretzels and items missing here and there, so I clung to her steady arm everywhere we went. She without a child and I without a mom.

One day at the beach, she watched me playing with my brothers and sisters in the sand, watched my face as the other children dug their granted toes into the fleece of a summer day, and waded nonchalantly in the foam. She saw the green of envy in my eyes and caught the gently flooding tears of knowing I would never dangle from the jungle gyms of easy motion. Florence was scared to death of water and had never learned to swim, yet she swept me up in her loving arms and carried me into the surf I could not navigate alone. "You haven't a spring in your step, my dear, so you must have one in your heart," she used to say. Together, we dipped what toes I had in the milk of the waves. She felt with me the stinging stares of passersby who always asked, "Dear God! What happened to your leg?"

One morning I awoke and rubbed my sleepy eyes. On the floor beside my bed was a dollhouse, a mansion really; she had designed and built it as I slept. Replete with curtains, carpets, silken chaise, a mahogany dresser, a four-poster bed with a canopy, and a miniature tea set made of bone china the color of lapis, which matched her dancing eyes. We played and played and played in this house of dreams, rearranging the furniture again and again and again; our nimble fingers never clashed. She taught me what it was to waltz without a pair of legs. In our palace, we sipped tea with Emily in her English garden or served a luncheon for the Queen.

When I was old enough to listen, she read me the sonnets of Shakespeare and Milton, each stanza a song as she spoke. But what rises above the syllables is the perfect rhythm and rhyme of how she gave and gave and gave. It's been almost three years since her death, and I can still smell the scent of Nina Ricci in her hair, hear her laughter ringing in my ears, and feel the cameo of her gentle heart in mine.

JANET I. BUCK TEACHES WRITING AND LITERATURE AT THE COLLEGE LEVEL AND IS WIDELY PUBLISHED IN JOURNALS, E-ZINES, AND ANTHOLOGIES AROUND THE WORLD. HER POETRY SITES ON THE WEB HAVE RECEIVED MORE THAN THIRTY AWARDS.

TRULY LIBERATED

Elaine Beale

 was eighteen and I sat in my grandmother's living room, sipping tea from one of her best china cups and showing off my university-acquired vocabulary by lecturing her on the importance of feminism and sexual (not that I ever used *that* word in front of her) politics. "Don't talk to me about women's liberation," she said, brushing cake crumbs from the corner of her mouth. "I've never needed liberating in my life." I couldn't help nodding.

Grandma was no revolutionary, nor did she escape the hardship and drudgery that befell women of her class and generation. She was born poor, stayed poor, and raised ten children through the Depression and World War II. When I was a child, I loved to listen to stories about her life. "Tell me about the olden days, Grandma," I'd say, looking up to her wide, saggy face with broken veins across her cheeks. She'd nod, shuffle down in her chair, and describe what it was like to grow up near the docks, running barefoot in the winter down cobbled streets when they heard a ship had come in. "Of course, my dad never liked us going there. He'd give us a belting if he found out. He was a bit of a sadist, your great-granddad." She told me how she loved school and, at fourteen, it was her dream to become a teacher. "I could have got a scholarship, but it was different then." She sighed and pursed her thin lips. "You had no choice, you had to go out and earn a wage." She told me about marrying at sixteen, having three babies before she was twenty, how she considered herself lucky to be able to afford disinfectant when the midwife came, how she lost all her teeth before she was thirty. And she talked about the war, how she quite liked it when all the men went away, how she kept a kitchen knife under her pillow to fight off the Germans.

As I grew up, it never crossed my mind that older women were over the hill. My grandmother was a firestorm of energy. She ran the local Women's Institute with the drive of a dictator of a small state. She organized jumble sales and fund-raisers for the church, baked pies for harvest festivals, summer fairs, spring events. She went ballroom dancing, played bingo, read voraciously, made her own dresses, sweaters, bead curtains, quilts, antimacassars, tablecloths, and handled with ease the hordes of friends and family who regularly descended on her household. She welcomed all of her twenty-five grandchildren with hugs that buried us in the comfort of her flowery perfume, her soft and fleshy arms, her unconditional affection.

She never held back from expressing her opinions. She loved royalty, hated waste, couldn't understand "all these new-fangled fashions, and that noise they call music nowadays." When I went to visit, we couldn't walk to the corner store without at least three people stopping her to talk. "This is my grandbairn," she'd say, beaming down at me. "She's bonny, don't you think? And, like me, she's got a good head on her shoulders." It was all the compliment I ever needed.

Grandma was the linchpin for the entire family. I bought the family myth and believed she would live forever. When she died, at the age of eighty-four, not only could

I not absorb the shock, but I also lived with the terrible regret of not having been back to England to visit her in over four years. It wasn't that I didn't think of her, I just relied on her always being there—like the sky and the stars, or the hard, reassuring earth beneath my feet. Now, when I suddenly remember that she's not there any longer, I still find myself sobbing. But I find comfort in the thought that maybe she's still around, somewhere in the great beyond, truly liberated.

ORIGINALLY FROM ENGLAND, ELAINE BEALE IMMIGRATED TO THE UNITED STATES IN 1989. HER FIRST NOVEL, *MURDER IN THE CASTRO,* WAS PUBLISHED BY NEW VICTORIA IN 1997. SHE CURRENTLY LIVES IN OAKLAND, CALIFORNIA.

THE POWER OF WISDOM

Susan M. Janes

or an entire childhood and until my wedding day, when I walked the aisle into the care of my new husband, my grandmother protected me from my parents' full capacity for cruelty. She greeted my groom warmly that day, then tilted toward him to pronounce through her teeth, "Be good to Susan or I will kill you."

My grandmother's heritage shaped me during my first seven years, when we lived in her home. Three hundred years ago, with Calvinist Reformation burning in their souls, her Scottish kin immigrated to America. They valued honest, hard work, rather than wealth; dignified, honorable, and moral living, rather than higher education; leadership and responsible citizenship, rather than power.

My unhappiness began when Mother and her new husband moved away from my grandmother. I had to use my stepfather's name without being adopted, and keep my mother's divorce a secret. That summer, my own father and his new wife disappeared forever into a distant city to begin their life without me.

Coping with second-class status became my greatest ongoing challenge, once the "real" daughters were born. Periodically, I ran away to my grandmother's house, per-

Winnie
Mayes
Nisbett

haps after a long Saturday of scrubbing bathrooms, ironing, folding laundry, waxing floors, dusting, changing beds, and washing dishes alone. My parents' refusal to drive me to a friend's for a sleepover or to share the driving to a movie, sent me running to my grandmother for solace. When I learned to drive, I chauffeured my young sisters, but could not use the car for my own social activities. One Saturday in high school, I missed the fun of decorating the gym for the prom, because no matter what, I was on nonstop call for nonstop chores. Finally there was the wedding they would not give me, but later gave to their "real" daughters. The only family member who contributed to the joy of the day was my grandmother, who hosted a luncheon for the bridal party.

I'd arrive at my grandmother's, sick with helplessness. She'd listen at her small kitchen table, attentively holding on to my distress. Turning my words over in her mind, she chose hers carefully. She never declared a guilty party, or offered advice on how to get along. Her words did not change my world. Instead, they freed me from entanglement within my mother's and stepfather's parental traps by pointing over their heads into my future. "Susan, when you have your own family someday, you can make it different."

The encompassing embrace of her memory remains my guide and strength. Sometimes, in a dream, we sit across from each other in a familiar room. She is old, fragile, and unable to speak, but words are unnecessary. In her presence I am protected, courageous, kind. I am utterly still, so that her fragile presence will linger. Just as I slip from my dream, I reach toward the hem of her simple housedress to touch the miracle of her presence in my life.

SUSAN M. JANES GREW UP IN ST. LOUIS, MISSOURI, AND GRADUATED FROM WASHINGTON UNIVERSITY WITH A B.S. IN ZOOLOGY AND AN M.A. ED. IN SCIENCE EDUCATION. AT AGE FIFTY-FIVE AND AFTER YEARS OF TEACHING SECONDARY-SCHOOL SCIENCE, SHE LIMITS HER COMMITMENTS TO TWO LOVES: HER FAMILY AND WRITING. SHE RESIDES IN GLENCOE, ILLINOIS, WITH HER HUSBAND, JAY, IN THE HOUSE IN WHICH THEY REARED THEIR TWO CHILDREN, EMILY AND ANDREW.

GRAND-MOTHER EARTH

WINTER LESSONS

Kate Boyes

ast night a storm swept through our valley, dropping a deep blanket of snow. At first light today, I break a path to the woodshed and split maple for the fire. Dry wood is already stacked inside by the stove, but I can't resist being out on a winter morning.

When snow falls, I think of my grandmother. She died last June, during an odd storm that covered much of the country with snow. She taught me how to live close to the earth and appreciate all its benefits, even the benefits of winter.

I remember complaining constantly about winter weather when I was young. Patiently, my grandmother would tell me people prayed for snow and freezing temperatures when she was a child. Back then, snow-packed roads made travel easy. Just a frozen crust along which sleighs flew like the wind.

Perhaps because I disliked winter so much, my grandmother gave me the carriage robe she'd used to cover her legs on sleigh rides. The robe is woven of soft wool. Four times since it came from the loom, a grandmother has passed the robe to her granddaughter. Through world wars, flu epidemics, house fires, and floods, each granddaughter has protected the robe.

I want to honor my grandmother during the weather she taught me to love, so I decide to freshen the robe. I carry it outside, lay it on clean snow, and kneel beside it. "Rub the flakes in gently," my grandmother used to say, showing me how with her chapped hands. "Wait for a cold day, around zero, so the snow won't melt. That's how to care for precious wool." As I rub snow into the fabric, the sadness of my grandmother's death loosens from the warp and weft. When I give the robe a hard shake, snow and sadness blow away.

Back inside, I sit in the rocker and wrap the robe around me. The wool smells clean and alive. I imagine the robe's first owner draping it over her legs, then taking the sleigh reins and driving her horses straight across a snow-covered prairie. I expect she thought the robe would be hers forever. Then she grew older, gave up winter carriage rides, and passed the robe to her granddaughter.

Until today, I thought I would hold the robe, as I wanted to hold my grandmother, forever. I didn't understand that my hands are just one pair in a long line of wind-chapped hands that have cherished and preserved the fabric of my family. I didn't understand that I care for what is precious so I can pass it along.

My grandmother wanted me to appreciate more than winter when she gave me the robe. She wanted me to appreciate this: Though I can hold nothing forever, the act of letting go weaves me more closely to my family.

I rock away through the winter afternoon, comforted by this warm thought.

KATE BOYES, AGE FORTY-FIVE, WRITES BY THE LIGHT OF KEROSENE LAMPS AND CANDLES. HER NATURE ESSAYS HAVE BEEN PUBLISHED IN SEVERAL ANTHOLOGIES. KATE TEACHES WRITING AT SOUTHERN UTAH UNIVERSITY.

GRANDMA'S CELLAR DOOR

DeMar Regier

he worn, weather-beaten cellar door slanted in such a way that its top, about a foot high, made an ideal ledge on which Grandma and I could sit. We observed the barn across the road, the outlying fields dotted with farm animals, the graceful willows near the house, and the wide expanse of prairie sky that stretched in every direction. Like two birds perched on a low limb, Grandma and I talked about all the happenings around us, or sat quietly, happy to be part of it all.

There, close to Grandma's side, listening to her observations and wise questions, I learned about life and the lessons that nature can teach. Our times together began with the first warm days and continued throughout the long days of harvest and late summer.

In the spring, the farmyard teemed with newborns. We watched the antics of a colt whose wobbly legs barely kept him upright, the proud mother duck as she led her ducklings to the creek, the frisky lamb greedily nursing. The lessons were clear: Get up when you're down; follow those who know where they're going; don't wolf your food.

I liked the birds. The bubbly trill of the house wren, the sad sounds of a whip-poorwill, the clear notes of a meadowlark were distinct. We talked about how their songs described them and how they resembled people: lazy cowbirds, busybody blue jays, meddling sparrows.

During harvest time, while we examined ripening kernels of wheat, Grandma told me about our Mennonite ancestors, how they brought turkey-red wheat to Kansas from Russia, and how the women sewed pockets filled with grain in all their garments to plant in the new land. I learned how important little seeds are; how women and men shared the work; how it takes time to grow.

And then there were Grandma's questions and comments. When she said, "That's a crimson sunset. There'll be no rain tomorrow." "It's so still. A storm is on the way." How did she know? Or when she asked, "Which stars would you like over your bed?" I pondered.

In time, the old cellar door was replaced by school doors, but nothing ever supplanted the heritage of Grandma's wisdom, wonder, and love of nature.

DeMar Regier of Prairie Village, Kansas, grew up learning to cherish the mysteries of nature, the close ties of relationships, the spirituality of solitude. Memories of Grandmother reaffirm those values; writing for children keeps the memories alive.

GOLDA

Mary Earle

he was Texas born and Texas bred. She survived the Galveston hurricane of 1900, the Great Depression, and over fifty years of marriage to my grandfather. This was no small feat. Golda Willis Kopecky was a maverick. She took off for Galveston in order to become a nurse, leaving behind a conventional life. She fell in love with and married a man who was a Bohemian. She went where her heart led, even when that was risky, even when that was against the grain.

She was a mystic in her own way—not the sort of mystic of whom weighty hagiography is penned. Not the sort of mystic whose feats of sanctity leave the rest of us wondering if the person was really human. The wonder of life and the mystery of love were at the center of Golda's living. Early on, I became

145

aware of her morning ritual. She would traipse across the grass, garden hose in hand, and water the plants. To the casual eye this appeared to be a chore. To some of us, this was revealed to be an act of worship. Her presence showed us what prayer looked like; we children saw reverence and delight in this daily connection to earth. Golda would stand in the garden, blessing the dripping leaves, noting the changes, rooting herself and her family in what Marge Piercy has called " the common, living dirt"—the earth that is our home and our mother.

Golda taught me to feed the earthworms. Every morning, she would put coffee grounds, banana peels, and other vegetable bits in the garden by the back door. Those worms, well fed and tended, created rich soil, dark and aromatic. The toads that lived under Golda's back stoop were equally well treated; she made sure there was fresh water for their drinking. The "common, living dirt" was home—home for worms, for toads, for vegetables. This earth home was dear and sacred.

When I was about six, several of us grandkids were gathered at Golda and Joe's ranch near Borne in the Texas hill country. We were playing underneath the water tower, dancing around in sheets of cascading water. Suddenly Golda emerged from the cedar trees at the lip of the canyon. She emerged radiant and astonishingly beautiful. Her hands waved in the air. She searched for words. "I have been given such a gift! I saw two king snakes doing their dance!" The air around her pulsed, quivered. We grandchildren became mute. Now I know that we were beholding that age-old, bone-deep knowing: Fall down and worship. Take off your shoes. Keep silence. Keep watch.

I was beholding ecstasy.

From that moment on, I began to awaken to the truth that the earth is holy ground.

MARY EARLE, FORTY-NINE, IS THE OLDEST GRANDDAUGHTER OF THE KOPECKY/ COLBERT TRIBE. SHE IS AN EPISCOPAL PRIEST, POET, TEACHER, AND RETREAT LEADER AND RESIDES IN SAN ANTONIO, TEXAS. HER WORK HAS BEEN PUBLISHED IN *ANAMCHAIRDE*, *THE SOLITARY LIFE*, AND *THE TEXAS JOURNAL OF IDEAS* AND IN DIOCESAN AND NATIONAL CHURCH PUBLICATIONS.

Eva Wolberg

Golda Willis
Kopecky

MY GRANDMOTHER'S TEARS

Lisa M. Fisher

When I was eight, my friends bragged about their grand-mothers' homemade cookies. My grandmother, Eva, was mixing acidophilus cultures and explaining proper yoga breathing.

When my grandfather died, everyone began to bring sick plants to Grandma Eva. I couldn't miss the sudden increase: aloe, coleus, jade.

"Where did this one come from?" I'd ask.

"Oh, this one was your Aunt Charlotte's," she'd say.

I noticed the thick leaves on the jade; vibrant, purple flowers exploding from the formerly sickly African violet dropped off by Cousin De De. Soon there were leaves overlapping every powder-blue, wrought iron table on her sunporch.

Here I learned about cuttings, how you could take the broken shoots, submerge them stem down in water until roots grew long and strong enough to be replanted. I watched her trim dead leaves, water and rotate, ensuring proper sunlight. Miraculously all the plants grew strong; sprouting shoots, new buds, and flowers. Tears filled her eyes when she'd speak of living things: flowers, birds, and family.

As I followed her around the porch helping her tie back weighted branches of the rubber tree; I started to ask questions I'd never asked anyone before. "Do you believe in life after death?" I was curious. What did she dream of late at night in the big, empty house? "His arms were outstretched, and he was calling for me," she'd say, referring to my grandfather. My grandmother's voice quivered and her milky blue eyes, damaged from cataracts, filled with tears as she smiled. "He was so close . . . I could almost feel him."

My grandmother Eva is now 101 years old. She sits quietly on the sunporch, blind and partially deaf. She stares out to a place in the backyard I can't see. She smiles and hugs me. I've noticed the tears for the last twenty-five years, the way they come when she hugs me as I enter the house, the way her eyes fill when she says, "God bless you," and somehow I feel truly blessed. Tears when we sit in the porch having her homemade vegetable barley soup, toast and sweet butter, and sliced apple for dessert.

Like my grandmother, I too cry over the simplest things: driving home from the grocery store and witnessing clouds rolling across the late-afternoon pink sky; thinking of my children or the kindness in a stranger's smile; buds on tree branches; the miracle of finding a peregrine falcon perched on a dead oak branch as I pull into my driveway.

I've asked her what the secret of life is. She laughs and says, "Never stop moving. Exercise every day. Eat plenty of fruits and vegetables." What she never says with words, I can read in her tear-filled eyes. Her secret, and now mine, is to live each day in awe.

LISA MARKS FISHER OF LAKE FOREST, ILLINOIS, HAS PUBLISHED FICTION AND POETRY IN A NUMBER OF JOURNALS, INCLUDING *FARMERS MARKET, ROCKFORD REVIEW,* AND *ECRIVEZ.* SHE HAS ALSO PUBLISHED IN TWO ANTHOLOGIES *A LOVING VOICE.*

ONE HUNDRED WINTERS

Liesel Litzenburger

 have a photograph of my great-grandmother standing in Mackinaw City, Michigan, in 1908. It is winter and she is wearing a long dark coat and resting her gloved hand on the handle of the little sled her baby, my grandmother, rests in, buried under a thick pile of blankets. Behind them, far off in the distance, there are a few small buildings, maybe houses, and then only whiteness as far as the eye can see. The whiteness, of course, is snow. So much snow that it isn't hard to imagine there is not another living thing for miles and miles.

Sometimes when I hold this photograph up close and study the expression on my great-grandmother's face, a look of pioneer steeliness and shy beauty, I wonder what it was that brought her to this place, so far from what might have been an easier life, and what it was that made her stay.

Three generations later I am here, close to where my great-grandmother stood still for a moment eighty-nine years ago. I was born and raised in northern Michigan, and I find myself living and working here again, after several years away. People like to say that everything has changed up north and it has, even in the short time I've lived elsewhere. But something important remains exactly the same: the same landscape, the same snow, the same air so cold it sometimes makes my chest ache. The women in my family collectively have made it through more than one hundred of these winters. Just as I wonder what made my great-grandmother choose to remain here, this winter I began to wonder what makes me stay in a place so beautiful yet remote, so stark and simple, a place that is both easier and harder to love than so many other places.

The writer Roland Merullo said: "You loved or hated a place because you loved or hated yourself in that place." So the truth is that maybe we are most ourselves, for better or for worse, in the place we call home. It is something she must have known, that this northern landscape, even in winter, makes us who we are.

Today, my grandmother, the blanket-swaddled baby in the photograph, is ninety years old. She lives happily on her own in a house looking out at Lake Michigan. When I talk to her, she tells me about the way the snow is falling that day or about the way the ducks have flocked in a great circle on the dark waters out beyond her windows. She has learned to watch and wait, knowing a simple fact I had somehow forgotten: that soon enough the clouds will lift, the drifts will fade, the budded trees will open again. The world will be a little easier to love.

LIESEL LITZENBURGER, THIRTY-ONE, WRITES FICTION AND NONFICTION. SHE RECEIVED HER M.F.A. FROM WESTERN MICHIGAN UNIVERSITY AND TEACHES ENGLISH AT THE UNIVERSITY OF MICHIGAN.

Hazel Reycraft

Julia Rambam

THE BETSY ROSS OF SOUTH FLORIDA

Merril Mushroom

hey call her "The Betsy Ross of South Florida" because she stitches such beautiful flags. It's wartime, early 1940s, and she runs the Red Cross sewing room in Miami. Because she's my grandma, I get to go there with her sometimes. I play with fabric, buttons, and thread that she gives me. One time, a Norwegian ship is torpedoed off the coast of Miami, and the survivors are brought to my grandma at the Red Cross to have new uniforms made. These men are so tall, and my grandma is so tiny, that she has to climb up and down a stepladder to measure them.

Grandma opens her home to servicemen from the many military bases in South Florida. These boys are conditioned to pride in fighting for democracy, but their fear is lurking, and they miss their mothers. Some of them will die soon in the war. Grandma's family saves their ration coupons all week long so that grandma can cook for the boys on the weekends and feed them well.

After the war, as the number of her grandchildren increases, Grandma feeds us well, too. We go to her home—aunts, uncles, cousins, second cousins—every Sunday and on all the major holidays.

Often I find her working outside in her garden when we come to visit. She keeps a dish towel hanging around her neck so that she can wipe the perspiration off her face before she kisses us. Grandma is very thoughtful. Sometimes when I stay with her, she gives me spoons and lets me dig in the dirt of her garden while she works nearby.

Grandma is dead a long time now. I miss her. I've tried my hand at sewing, but I never was any good at it, just did not have the eye or the patience. But I love to cook and to feed my friends and my family, and sometimes I open my home to strangers.

Most of all, I love to garden. I feel Grandma with me often when I hoe the dirt, dig the ground, prune the shoots, and nurture the yield from the earth. In my garden, I turn up memories of the sweet-smelling days of my childhood, as I sit on the ground turning moist soil onto the roots of newly set plants, while Grandma works nearby, her dish towel around her neck, smiling over at me every now and again.

MERRIL MUSHROOM IS A JEWISH WRITER WHO LIVES IN RURAL TENNESSEE AND GROWS A BIG GARDEN. SHE WAS BORN IN 1941 IN SOUTH FLORIDA. SHE BECAME A GRANDMOTHER IN 1997.

MARTHA

Joanne Pieza McGlone

he only grandmother I knew was a simple peasant woman who wore cotton housedresses and a babushka. Martha pulled her white hair back with two combs and tied it in a small knot. She wore two small gold earrings and a gold wedding band on her hand. Her strong hands, covered with wrinkled skin and lined with black creases, told her story.

As a young girl she went to the fields to labor instead of going to school in her native Lithuania. As a young woman she left her home and her family to sail steerage to America. She never saw her family again.

This humble woman felt a responsibility to nurture and preserve the earth. She was an environmentalist before this word made an entrance into our familiar vocabulary. When I helped her to wash the dinner dishes, we used two pans of hot water that we boiled on the wood-burning stove. We used no soap because the dishwater was dumped into the yard and Grandmother said we could not pollute the soil with soapy water.

I especially liked to walk to the potato field with Grandmother to remove potato bugs from the plants. We dropped the doomed invaders into a can filled with kerosene. Pesticides were not used in this field. I can still see my grandmother bent over the rows of plants, a kind mistress in this undulating field of green, her apron blowing in the refreshing evening winds. Sheltered under waning summer clouds fading to some other place, surrounded by the mesmerizing scent of lilac bushes in bloom, listening to the good-night twitters of bobwhites settling down in their idyllic field nests, she spoke to me in Lithuanian, and I answered in English. There she taught me so many lessons about caring for the precious earth.

Inherent in her nature was a spirituality that caused her to always communicate with her God. She was His daughter nurturing His earth. Whenever I pick up a shovel and push that first thrust into the spring earth, I feel my grandmother's presence, and a connection to her through this newly awakened and fragrant ground. We share again those days of working in the field together and there is a continuity in spirit.

JOANNE MARTHA PIEZA MCGLONE, SIXTY, LIVES IN HAZEL CREST, ILLINOIS. SHE IS A HOMEMAKER, SUBSTITUTE GRAMMAR-SCHOOL TEACHER, AND AVID GARDENER. SHE AND HER HUSBAND, JOHN, HAVE BEEN MARRIED FOR THIRTY-NINE YEARS AND HAVE ONE DAUGHTER, FIVE SONS, AND TEN GRANDCHILDREN.

SNAPSHOTS
in
TIME

NANA

Karen Benke

She takes her walk up the hill each day, stopping on her way down
at the corner market, where she shops for my visit, for the mid-day meal
we will share. Later, in her yellow kitchen, I watch her drizzle olive oil
over eggplant, pasta, long loaves of bread, and when she sees me,
she reaches for my shoulders, then ushers me to the chair in the dining room
where Papa once sat. Handling me bowl after bowl, she fills my glass
with red wine and points to the wild roses that grow along the fence,
as the wind blows waves across her careful garden. Then, smiling shyly,
she disappears into the kitchen again, returning with the biscotti
she has saved from her last trip to Italy. "What else can I get for you, Angel?"
she asks, pouring my tea, her brown eyes taking me in.
How do I tell her she has given me everything already?
All of her love on porcelain plates, spread across white linen.

KAREN BENKE'S POEMS AND STORIES HAVE APPEARED IN A VARIETY OF PERIOD-ICALS AND ANTHOLOGIES, INCLUDING *CQ: CALIFORNIA QUARTERLY, PLOUGHSHARES, ARTISTS DIALOGUE, AN INTRICATE WEAVE: WOMEN WRITE ABOUT GIRLS AND GIRLHOOD* AND THE FORTHCOMING *MOTHER'S NATURE: TIMELESS WISDOM FOR THE JOURNEY INTO MOTHERHOOD.* A RECIPIENT OF GRANTS FROM THE MARIN ARTS COUNCIL, *POETS & WRITERS,* AND THE HEDGEBROOK FOUNDATION, SHE TEACHES PRIVATELY AND IN THE CALIFORNIA POETS IN THE SCHOOLS PROGRAM. SHE IS THIRTY-THREE AND LIVES WITH HER HUSBAND IN MILL VALLEY.

Nina Grandi
Nelson

A KEEPER

Jennifer Drake Dent

ust wrap one hand around like this and the other hand on the line. Wiggle him around a bit . . . and Walah! A keeper!" Gramma tossed my six-inch bluegill into the bucket with the five she had already caught and tossed her line back into the lake.

Every night we fished after dinner. Grampa went out in the boat, and me and Gramma stayed on the dock. We tried all going out in the boat together one night. But when I pulled my line up and swirled it around like I was trying to lasso a bull and instead captured Gramma's fishing pole, my trips in the boat were brought to an abrupt end. "That's OK," Gramma laughed. "We'll just fish from the dock."

And so we did. Each evening around six-thirty, we'd grab the bait from the refrigerator, put on my life jacket, and descend the hilly path to the lake.

We didn't talk much. You had to be quiet on the Lake because your voices would carry and disrupt the people fishing. So we sat on the bench at the end of the dock, a five-gallon bucket at our feet, and a paper cup full of maggots between us, patiently watching for our bobbers to drop below the surface of the water.

Gramma fished with maggots. "They're cleaner than night crawlers," she said. I always giggled when we opened the lid on the cup, and they slithered around trying to escape our prying fingers. It's as if they knew that their destiny lay on the end of a hook. "Shh," Gramma would say, "You don't want to disturb the others." But I could tell she wanted to laugh, too.

In the morning we would wake early, pull a hooded sweatshirt over our night-gowns, and creep quietly onto the front porch. Gramma would sip her coffee while I ate sticky glazed doughnuts and drank hot milk, and we would watch the clearing in hopes of seeing a mother doe and her family eating their morning meal.

Our days were always somehow filled. We would walk the dirt roads looking for flowers to match the ones we read about in the wildflower book. Or try and catch a close-up glimpse of the hummingbirds coming up to the feeder on the porch. One day, we were exploring the woods and Gramma took off her shoes, rolled up her pants, and stepped in the water of the creek. "Let's go to the other side," she urged, already halfway across. I quickly shed my blue Keds and tube socks, rolled up the legs of my overalls, and followed closely behind. Gramma always led me in the right direction.

"Another keeper," she said as she cleaned the fish off my hook. She tossed it in the bucket, rebaited my hook, and handed me my pole. I watched closely, detailing her every move, and hoping someday, I would be able to do it all just like Gramma. I threw my line out near hers and waited.

JENNIFER DRAKE DENT, TWENTY-SEVEN, TEACHES HIGH-SCHOOL ENGLISH IN JACKSONVILLE, FLORIDA. SHE ENJOYS RUNNING, READING, WRITING, AND TRAVELING.

DOUBLEMINT AND MINK

Sharyn L. Bolton

he beauty shop was glass, white uniforms, and a Coke machine that sold chubby six-ounce colas for six cents. My grandmother, calling herself a "beautician," ruled that universe. And on the days I was allowed to visit her, I reigned with her in that glamorous world where the famous and infamous women of Memphis encouraged my smiles.

At day's end, Nannie locked the doors and dimmed the lights. A chill settled and the aftermath of permanent-wave solution fogged the air. Nannie covered her pristine nylon with a full-length mink coat and tossed a brightly colored scarf around her neck.

Once inside her car, before turning on the ignition, she took out a stick of Doublemint and split it in half, a treat to share on the trip to my grandparents' farmhouse, miles outside the city limits. Cuddled next to the luxuriant fur, I concentrated on cracking and popping my gum, striving for my grandmother's skill level. Then Nannie's gentle, drawling words cascaded down to me.

"Baby, the house was huge, white columns and a front porch that stretched from yonder and back. When you stepped inside, it was like another world. Persian carpets and tapestry. Did I tell you they had a butler in a white starched coat?" As she described her recent visit to a customer's house, I stretched the gum over my tongue, released it, filled it with air, drew it back, and sucked quickly, releasing a loud popping sound.

Johnnie
Bolton

Nannie smiled and imitated my efforts.

"Tea sandwiches and delicate flowered porcelain cups. Laid out, just for me," she continued.

For a moment there were only car sounds, the putting of the engine, heat wafting from the floorboards, and traffic swooshing alongside.

"Wait till I tell you, baby. Lord help us to get right. They up and called their race-horse after you."

"Really, Nannie, really?"

"I do declare. A racehorse named for my baby."

"Did you see her? You know, the horse?"

"A beauty. Sleek and regal. A Tennessee Walker, maybe. She's a winner alright."

With the visual images of grace, hooves striking the ground, a yoke of yellow flowers, I forgot to crack my gum as I nestled in the welcoming cushion of mink. Shadows played with the sunlight as we drove across the countryside nearer to the farm. Storytime would give way to Papa's greeting, then the normality of fixing supper.

"Nannie, tell me again about you and Papa eloping."

"Lawdy, child. You've heard that story a dozen times."

Her words sparkled with the telling. I could imagine her chestnut hair whipping behind her as she sat beside Papa, who rode tall on the buggy seat and cracked the whip in the air, urging the horse to higher speeds. As they raced across the Mississippi farmlands, my great-grandpa gave chase. Still, they reached the justice of the peace before him.

Cracking my Doublemint gum and warmed by a blanket of mink, I listened in wonder, engrossed by the power of words, envisioning my writer's dream.

SHARYN L. BOLTON IS STILL INTRIGUED BY THE POWER OF WORDS AND PERSONAL HISTORY. AS A PSYCHOLOGIST, FREELANCE WRITER, AND MOTHER OF TWO ADOLESCENTS, SHE INCORPORATES HER GRANDMOTHER'S LEGACY—TO LISTEN, OBSERVE, AND FREE THE IMAGINATION.

AN EXAMPLE TO LIVE BY

Sonia Millard

ithin seconds the race was on. The wind blew my hair back away from my face. The landscape rolled by in a blur. My only thought was that I had to catch up to my friend. My legs pushed harder on the pedals.

Then, without warning, a rock in the road sent me reeling out of control. The bike stopped, and I kept going. I could feel the hot gravel as it embedded itself in my skin.

Pain seared through my body as I came to a sudden halt. I looked at my bloodied hands and legs in shock. The race was over.

Slowly and painfully I got to my feet. I looked up the hill to Grandma's house. That's where I needed to go. Leaving my bike, I started up the hill. What had taken only seconds to go down, now seemed to take hours to climb back up.

As I entered the coolness of the kitchen, I heard Grandma's intake of breath. "What happened to you?" came the inevitable question.

She put me in a chair and wiped away my tears. I knew she would take care of me.

Within minutes, she seated herself across from me with needle in hand. This was something she had done many times. I watched her hands as she worked the gravel out of my hands and knees. You could see a lifetime of work and caring in her fingers.

I remember wishing for hands like Grandma's. Hands that knitted blankets and took care of babies. Hands that hung laundry out to dry and planted flowers in the rock garden. Hands that helped other people and just made you feel loved.

Grandma finished her work and applied a cool ointment that helped ease the pain. I don't remember how but suddenly I was lying in Grandma's giant waterbed and thinking it was the most comfortable place in the whole world. I was still hurting, but I felt safe in the dark and cool room. I knew Grandma was there.

That day so long ago was one of many days that my grandmother was there to love and support me.

I still draw on the example she set for me. During the times in my life when I lose all patience and I feel like giving up, I wonder what Grandma would do. When I feel like I will never finish something, I remember that Grandma finished school while taking care of five children. When I grieve the loss of a loved one, I remember that Grandma lost her parents, her siblings, and even a child. I know that I will make it through, just as she did.

A woman who spent her life serving others, Grandma is everything I hope to be.

SONIA MILLARD, TWENTY-THREE, HAS AN ASSOCIATE DEGREE IN PHOTOGRAPHY FROM MOHAWK VALLEY COMMUNITY COLLEGE. SHE WORKS WITH PEOPLE WITH DISABILITIES AT UNITED CEREBRAL PALSY ASSOCIATION. SHE ENJOYS HIKING, ARTS AND CRAFTS, AND READING.

GIFTS ETERNAL

C. J. Johnson

ranma, hurry up and open this door. The afternoon sun is hot. I can smell those yummy sugar cookies. I can't wait to sink my teeth into them. Of course, cookies ain't the only reason I'm at Granma's door. Momma sent me on a mission to get some thread. Big Bro' walked with me the thirteen blocks. I kept telling Momma it is 1962, this is Watonga, Oklahoma, I am eight years old, and I can walk across town to Granma's by myself.

I love Granma missions. There is always a delicious smell to tickle your nose, entice your eyes, and squeeze your tummy. In the mornings Granma has big fat French biscuits; yesterday's biscuits dipped in egg batter and pan fried. When drenched in hot syrup, ain't nothing better. The thought makes my taste buds dance.

Evenings she is in the kitchen seasoning collard greens with fatback, making cracklin' cornbread and frying okra from Pappa's garden. The smells make my head swirl. I hated watching her wring the necks of them poor chickens, but they sure did taste good.

Granma never let company leave her house empty-handed. She gave them something from the garden or pantry. No matter how low her supplies. Neighbors knew they could count on Nellie.

Hurry up, Granma, and open the door. I walked across town by myself. I am eleven and don't need knucklehead Big Bro' to walk with me.

Today's mission is to help in the garden and bring home whatever Granma sends. Granma's lilac bushes are showing off and their sweet smell is pungent. As we tended peas, greens, and corn, I asked how she knew these seeds would make all this food.

She said, "Faith in God, Calin."

Oklahoma gets hot and humid quickly. I'm ready to go do indoor chores. Like jump on the bed—I mean, make the bed. Granma caught me jumping on the bed once. "Would you like if I jumped on your bed? You have to treat people and things the way you want to be treated."

Hurry up, Pappa, and open the door, it's me, Calin. Today, Granma is in her favorite rocking chair, quilting. I watch as she meticulously takes the needle in and out of pieces of Pappa's worn overalls and chambray shirts.

"Gal, pick up that crying baby. Give him a sugar cookie."

With a big sigh and a hug, I slow the rocking motion and tell Granma there is no baby crying. I hold her empty hands tightly in mine. There's no quilt in her lap, no needle or thread. Hardening of the arteries has robbed me of Granma. It has stolen my sugar cookies and French biscuits. It has shut down my busy bee granny. I hate this disease; it sends Granma out to the cotton fields or to draw water. It's 1970 and she hasn't lived on the farm for ten years. We have to keep the doors locked to keep Granma in.

Hardening of the arteries has packed away my granny but not my priceless gifts. She gave me her pretty smile, busy hands, warm heart, and my earth angel, Momma. She doesn't show recognition in her eyes, but I still bask in the warmth of her spirit.

C. J. Johnson walks the Four-Fold Path of Healer, Teacher, Warrior, and Visionary, which she practices through her writings and interactions with others. She is a cultural chaperon, inviting people of all ethnicity to celebrate our differences and embrace our commonalities. C. J. lives in Jonesboro, Georgia, and is a wife of twenty-six years and mother of two.

Nellie Jona Burton

TRUE LOVE

Ellen Holtzblatt

onia Asher was a woman who spoke her mind. She was "being honest, telling the truth," she would say. Many felt the sting of her "truths," myself included.

I would often tell Grandma that I loved her, to which she would reply, "Eh! What's love?" I knew that Grandma loved me, but the words "I love you" didn't dwell in her "truths." She had grown up poor and Jewish in anti-Semitic Czarist Russia. She entered a loveless marriage at the age of twenty-one. The concept of love was an alien language, rife with shadows and open spaces.

I possessed the stubbornness of youth and genes, so I continued to tell my grandmother that I loved her. To each earnest expression of my feelings, Grandma would reply with some variation of "Eh! What's love?" I would not be deterred. One day, I sat in my kitchen talking to Grandma on the phone. I said, "I love you," and received the response of "I love you too."

After that incident, Grandma never stopped saying "I love you"—it was in every birthday card she sent me, along with the traditional two dollars for a present. "I love you" soon became "I love you, darling." I remember feeling the power of my love. My love could create. My love could heal. My love could bridge. Maybe the other grand-children remember my grandmother's transformation as the result of the strength of their love. I never discussed it with them. I *knew* that it was my love that had worn her down to a different layer of truth.

Of course Grandma still offended people with her honesty. She still complained about her hearing aid, her glasses, her bad knees. She seemed to be the same woman, but she could forever after admit that she loved. During those later years, when the senility undid the woman that was, I visited her less and felt guilt more. Ours was not a perfect love, but it was true.

ELLEN HOLTZBLATT IS A FORTY-ONE-YEAR-OLD ARTIST AND MOTHER OF TWO INTELLIGENT, SENSITIVE, AND INTENSELY SILLY DAUGHTERS. SHE STRUGGLES TO MAKE SPACE IN HER TIME FOR ART BECAUSE LIFE SEEMS TO DEMAND OTHER THINGS OF HER. AT MOMENTS, WHEN ALL HER WORLDS FLOW INTO ONE BEING, SHE EXPERI-ENCES CLARITY OF VISION. SHE LOVES THOSE MOMENTS.

Sonia Asher

Mary Edna
Ripley Grosinsky

A LIFETIME OF
SERVICE

SuzAnne C. Cole

uge swollen knuckles, tissue-thin skin mottled with brown, fingers cruelly distorted and splayed at awkward angles, my grandmother's hands lie slackly in her lap. Wearily, they rise a few inches and then drop into her lap again. "God was really mean to me when he took away my hands," she says. "When I think of all the things these hands have done. . . . Now I'm an old woman of ninety-six, and not to be able to use my hands anymore is a cruel, cruel trick."

And we reminisce, she in her wheelchair, I on the little stool at her side, together, yet alone in our separate memories. I remember those hands . . .

Cracked and bleeding bringing in laundry frozen stiff by icy January winds on
the Kansas plains,
Rotating the handle of a wringer washer, squeezing the water from denim
overalls, worn workshirts, faded print feed-sack aprons and "mop" towels,
Dealing out cards for endless games of canasta on long winter nights and
Sunday afternoons,
Chopping wood and stoking the cast-iron stove from sullen-gray, early-morning
somnolence to a cheerful red-and-orange roar,
Darning socks late at night with coarse dark thread and a wooden darning egg,
Drawing yellow, tinny-tasting water from the cistern to fill the white
porcelain-enamel household buckets,
Grabbing a squawking chicken by the legs, beheading it in a shower of scarlet
and snow, plucking, scalding, gutting, frying it in home-rendered hog lard
and serving it crackling hot,
Wrapping a piece of sheeting around a finger whacked in a kitchen flurry to get
noon dinner on the table,
Stocking a grocery basket with all the treats we visiting grandchildren clamored
for—soda pop, wheels of longhorn cheese, Mallomars, sticky orange
"peanuts,"
Whopping the meanest bull on the farm with a piece of broken kindling to
drive him out of her kitchen garden,
Weeding, watering, harvesting, pickling, canning, and felling the produce from
that garden—a summer torture of sweat, dirt, chiggers, rashes, and steam-
filled kitchen for the winter pleasure of succulent squash, green beans, sour
and sweet pickles, corn, jams,
Bathing a baby or her aged mother with the same gentleness,
Cracking tenacious black walnuts with a hammer and staining her fingers
because somebody asked for her special black-walnut cookies.
Pointing out the wrestling "bad guy" on television while imploring the referee

to "look out, there, there, just see what he's doing" to her favorite in the white trunks.

What does she remember, sitting there and dreaming in her chair? Surely all that I remember and more. She turned fifty-two the day before I was born and always made me feel like her special belated birthday gift. Our family spent most holidays with Grandma Mary and Grandpa Elmer when I was growing up, and my cousins, brother, sister, and I usually visited their farm for two or three weeks every summer. During all those years, I never experienced her hands as less than loving as they tenderly guided mine as we rolled out dough, chopped vegetables, pumped water, and pulled weeds together.

Grandmother, it was a mean trick for arthritis to steal away the usefulness of your hands before you were ready to give up living and loving. May my hands be as dedicated to service as yours.

SUZANNE C. COLE, FIFTY-SEVEN, TAUGHT ENGLISH, FULL-TIME AND ADJUNCT, AT HOUSTON COMMUNITY COLLEGE FOR MORE THAN TWENTY YEARS. SHE'S PUBLISHED A BOOK OF MEDITATIONS, *TO OUR HEART'S CONTENT: MEDITATIONS FOR WOMEN TURNING 50* (CONTEMPORARY PUBLISHING COMPANY). SUZANNE'S WORK HAS APPEARED IN SEVERAL ANTHOLOGIES AS WELL AS IN NEWSPAPERS AND LITERARY MAGAZINES.

STAR

Joanne M. Clarkson

y grandmother Esther's name meant "star." She was small, dark, suspicious, curious, and superstitious. She and her sisters came to America from Sweden. Their English was broken and jobs were scarce. The three of them shared a bed in a boardinghouse in a poor neighborhood.

Ruth, the eldest, made friends with gypsies who camped in the alley behind them. They taught her to read fortunes, both palms and cards. She taught her sisters. With these skills and odd jobs, they survived.

Marguerite, the youngest, blond and curly-haired, with a fun-loving disposition, married early and had many children. Ruth died of consumption. Esther made her own way, working in a millinery shop. She seemed to know, with rose and ribbon, an occasional brooch or feather, how to make a woman beautiful. After a fitting, if a client requested it, she would do a discreet reading. In her own way, she was famous.

She had her idiosyncrasies. If she spilled salt, she threw a pinch over her left shoulder. If she forgot something and had to re-enter the house, she said, "Good luck" three times and sat on a chair. If she and a companion passed on either side of a light pole, they had to link little fingers and say, "Bread and butter." She married late and had one child, my mother, who was pretty, bright, and not one whit superstitious.

Of all the cousins, only I had an interest in the clairvoyant. My grandmother taught me, reluctantly at first. She rarely read the family. But when she saw that I had aptitude, we spent hours on the cards, rainy days in winter, deck spread across the card table. Summers on the back porch or under the cherry tree, aces scattered by wind. We bought new decks on holidays or when the spirit moved us.

And she would point out hands as we rode the bus, a crooked middle finger, a clubbed thumb. She traced my lines as though my life depended upon it. We checked out palmistry books from the public library and pored over photographs and diagrams.

She taught me to size up people and to retrace my life with red-and-black cards. She taught me to choose hearts and shun spades and all the ace of spades could mean besides death. She taught me that everything had meaning and that ritual has its place. I still can't resist a deck of cards. I judge by thumbs, the most important feature of a hand.

Our palms were not the same, hers small with pointed tips and close set thumbs. Mine larger, fingertips rounded and thumbs pointing out and away. I am the queen of hearts; she was queen of clubs. She was a star child; I am a child of earth. She died somewhat fearful and suspicious. From a more secure life, I am unafraid to use her tools to see into more dimensions. But if I forget something and have to come back into the house and no one is looking, I sit on a chair and whisper, "Good luck."

JOANNE M. CLARKSON, FORTY-EIGHT, LIVES IN SOUTHWESTERN WASHINGTON STATE. HER PUBLISHED WORK INCLUDES THREE CHAPBOOKS OF POETRY AND INDIVIDUAL POEMS AND NONFICTION ARTICLES APPEARING IN MORE THAN EIGHTY MAGAZINES AND JOURNALS.

Esther M. Erdman

Helena Rotzach

THE FACE THAT LAUNCHED A THOUSAND SHIPS . . .

Helen Schary Motro

y grandmother Helen was gassed in Treblinka in 1942. More accurately, presumed gassed. She might have suffocated on the transport train, or been peremptorily shot at the roundup spot on that autumn day when she vanished from the Warsaw Ghetto. She was among the victims to be snatched that fall when the Nazis began emptying the Ghetto in furtherance of their newly formalized, still-secret plan, their Final Solution.

I, Helen's namesake, was born six years afterward on another continent, worlds away.

For my mother, half a century later, the loss is yet a memory still too fresh. When I ask details of her mother's disappearance, she averts her gaze and talks of other things. And I wonder, *When she calls my name, is she also calling for her mother?*

So I, who never knew my grandmother, must reconstruct her life from the two blurry prewar photographs, which have miraculously survived, even though their subject did not. The first, taken in the '20s, shows a young woman on a trip to Paris. My grandmother Helen poses on a bench in Versailles, beside a marble urn among exquisite French gardens. Draped in a black shawl, with shining black eyes, my grandmother looks young, eager, composed, and provincial.

The second picture was taken on her balcony in Warsaw late in the 1920s. Helen has become a middle-aged woman with her hair in a careless bun, just looking up from work on her lap—a book? some sewing? The optimism of the 1920s is gone. War looms. My grandmother Helen seems to bear a premonition of her future. Here Helen is immediate, human, all too accessible. I can almost touch her vulnerability.

I am glad there is no record of her expression when she was herded at gunpoint.

As a child, I secretly wished my grandmother Helen back to life: I imagined that she would magically get out of a taxi in front of our apartment building; in my dream I would run up to show her where we lived.

I have been carrying forth Helen's memory all my life, this unknown, unsung woman who did not survive. I am approaching the age my young grandmother reached when she perished.

People used to assume I was named after Helen of Troy, but it is an altogether different kind of heroine I must live up to. In high school I was embarrassed when the boys laughingly quoted me poems about that Greek queen: I would never be a beauty icon. Now I know I have the harder task of memorializing another tragic Helen. And the only way to sing of my Helen is to be myself—and to live.

HELEN SCHARY MOTRO, BORN IN 1948, IS AN AMERICAN ATTORNEY AND WRITER LIVING IN ISRAEL AND NEW YORK.

MY GRANDMOTHER'S SOUL

Natasha Ware

They said I don't have
a grandma anymore,
and I answer, "But I do."
They say, "She died years ago."
They say she is underneath the ground.
I try not to cry,
and smile. "Yes, her *body* is beneath the ground,
but she is not."

"Her soul is in the wind
that blows the trees,
and the rolling rocks in the park."

"Grandma's soul is in the African mother's
breast, the breast that babies cry for."

I said, *"My daddy's momma's soul,* *it is not in the rich, thick,* *soil in a graveyard.*	*I know where my grandmother's soul is,* *it is in heaven."* *That's what I said.*

Dedicated to my grandmother Arlene.
"I love you, Grandma."

NATASHA WARE, TWELVE, IS A SECOND-YEAR STUDENT AT DENVER SCHOOL OF THE ARTS AS A CREATIVE-WRITING MAJOR. SHE IS A FORMER STUDENT AT SMITH SCHOOL OF THE ARTS ACADEMY. SHE KEEPS A 3.5 GRADE POINT AVERAGE, LOVES SCHOOL AND DRAMA, AND HOPES TO CONTINUE TO DO WHAT SHE DOES BEST—WRITE!

MOLLIE TREE

Reese Danley-Kilgo

It was a name that suited her.
She was tall, and straight, held her head
high. She walked firmly, but lightly
on the Alabama land she loved, had lived
on, for almost eighty years.

Tightly, she holds my hand in hers
as we walk, my grandmother and I,
past the pasture, by the barn,
through the field, down the hill.
It is June. Everything is summer green.
I am ten. I have been here every summer
of my life.

"Summer solstice," she says.
"The lightest, longest day. When it is
done,
the sun will turn. This is the day,
if we sit quietly here, we will hear
birdsong you will remember all your life."

"All the songs the birds have ever sung
are still here, in the leaves
of these trees. They can be heard again,
on this one day of summer, if you listen
long enough, if you sit here quiet
enough."

I remember, Mollie Tree. I remember you and me, walking, sitting on the bank of the Choctahatchee River, in the cool green shade, on the lightest, longest day of the year.

REESE DANLEY-KILGO, SEVENTY, IS A FORMER PROFESSOR AND FAMILY THERAPIST, NOW A WRITER, WHO ALWAYS WANTED TO BE A MOLLIE TREE KIND OF GRANDMOTHER AND NOW TRIES TO BE TO SUSANNA, NINE, BENJAMIN AND NICHOLAS (TWINS, FIVE), AND ERIKA, TWO. SHE LOVES PLANTS, POETRY, BOOKS, AND BABIES. HER NOVEL, *NINE BEAN ROWS,* WANTS A PUBLISHER.

GRANDMOTHER ANNIE B. OF ROCKY MOUNT, NORTH CAROLINA

Michelle Courtney Berry

nnie B. Williams was a broad-backed woman with strong hands and mother wit. She could run her fingers through barren fields and find crabgrass that removed the "stingers" from bee-stung skin. She could pluck four-leaf clovers, mix them with honey, and relieve any stomachache. Grandma even cured Aunt Irene of a rare disease after doctors had already issued the *There's-nothing-we-can-do-for-your-daughter* edict.

Grandma worked many jobs, raising six girls alone after her husband was murdered. Grandma Annie was a sharecropper, a house cleaner, and an entrepreneur. She even found time to don a uniform and work as a volunteer at the Red Cross during World War II. Grandma Annie was one of the few African-American volunteers in hospitals during that time.

Each summer I would leave the grit of New York City to visit her. She would meet me at the train station, smiling broadly, clutching a huge stuffed poodle. Not only did Grandma make her own line of stuffed animals, she also fashioned clothing for them. This particular poodle had trousers and a bright red bow at his neck.

After leaving the station, we walked to the drugstore, where Grandma bought me a hot dog with red onions and a Coca-Cola in a big glass bottle. She held my hand and told everyone I was her *grandbaby*. We laughed a lot.

Annie B. Williams

In the morning, I rose to hominy grits with dollops of butter, oven-baked buttered toast, fried bacon, scrambled eggs, and pork chops with gravy. At night we'd listen to the mysterious music of tree frogs and the clattering of crickets racing through the fields. She'd talk about speaking your mind, working hard, and the power of prayer. Grandma was a modern woman in an old-fashioned time.

When I was blackened by the North Carolina sun, plump beyond reason, and my New York accent had been traded for Southern slurring, Grandma gathered my things and took me to the train station. We boarded together, silent.

For hours, flashes of tobacco fields, glazed rivers, and green spaces would fill my thoughts. Sometimes she would sing. By the time the purple mountains glowed with fire and clouds gathered to usher in dusk, I was sleeping without sound, dreaming against Grandmother's arm.

MICHELLE COURTNEY BERRY, THIRTY-ONE, OWNS A MOTIVATIONAL SPEAKING AND TRAINING COMPANY. THE AUTHOR OF *THE MONTH OF NOT SPEAKING,* SHE IS A PERFORMANCE POET WHO USES STAND-UP COMEDY AND SONG TO ATTRACT DIVERSE AUDIENCES TO POETRY. A BUSINESS COLUMNIST AND AVID WRITER, BERRY APPEARS IN PLAYS AND COMMERCIALS. HER WORK HAS APPEARED IN *THE PATERSON LITERARY REVIEW, COKEFISH, AIM MAGAZINE, CELEBRATING VOICES: A FEMINIST REVIEW,* AND THREE CAVE CANEM POETRY ANTHOLOGIES.

A PARTY

Jeanne Quinn

emorial Day meant that I got to march in the parade with my nana. She belonged to the Spanish-American War Veterans auxiliary and I, at five, was allowed to tag along both to the parade and to meetings. She made me a white silk dress for the parade and a gold-and-red satin cape just like hers. I wore them proudly. She also let me carry a small American flag that usually dropped over one shoulder.

"Carry it straight," Nana admonished. "You'll poke someone's eye out."

Sometimes Nana took me to the auxiliary meetings. When we arrived at the hall, others were already setting up the chairs. The sounds of wooden chair legs scraping along the floor echoed in the empty room, mixing with the plunk of chair seats opening and old ladies chattering.

A voice from the podium called the meeting to order. The ladies' dresses rustled as they hurried to their seats. Voices drifted into murmurings and finally fell silent. The minutes were read, old business was taken care of, new business was announced. Crones nodded their heads "yea" or "nay," as the occasion required. Nana nodded her head along with the others. Afterward there would be tea and cake. Sitting next to my grandmother, I waited impatiently for the "afterward," squirming uncomfortably in the hard wooden chair.

Half dozing, totally disinterested, I watched the women stand, address the lady at the podium as "Madam President," make a motion, and then sit down. Someone else would stand, second the motion, and then everyone would vote. Would it ever end? I was hungry for tea and cake. At last, the end of the agenda was near. One more motion. Someone suggested a party.

A party? Suddenly I was all ears. Straightening in my chair, I waited for the second. It didn't come. I had no idea what the party was for or when it was going to be, but it was a party all the same. This I understood. This I cared about.

To my young impatience, there seemed to be an interminable silence between the motion for a party and a second. I fidgeted. No one came forward. The party was slipping away for want of a second. I stood up. "Madam President," I said, my child's voice barely audible in the vast room, "I second the motion." Satisfied with myself for following protocol, I sat down. The lady at the podium stared at me through thick glasses, the gavel in her hand suspended in midair, her mouth opened to speak. But all was silent. Not a word was uttered.

My grandmother, red faced, looked at me. She opened her mouth to speak, but nothing came out. A tittering started slowly in the back of the room, then grew to a crescendo. Chattering broke out, old ladies poked each other in the ribs and laughed. Amid the noise, someone seconded my second.

"Why ever did you do it?" Nana asked on the ride home from the meeting.

"For a party," I shrugged.

I don't remember the party. But always afterward, with mixed pride and mirth,

Nana told the story as though I had done something terribly bright. Ever afterward, she reinforced occasions when I spoke up for what I believed in.

As the years passed, Nana kept in touch by letter or phone, always with the same joy and enthusiasm I remembered in my youth. When she hugged me, I felt safe in her shelter, safe in her love.

I now have grandchildren of my own. Sometimes when I reach out to hug them, in my mind's eye I see her smiling and hugging me back.

JEANNE QUINN HAS WORKED AS A NEWSPAPER REPORTER, SPORTS PHOTOGRA-PHER, AND A BUYER FOR A BOOKSTORE. JEANNE IS ALSO A PUBLISHED POET. HER HUSBAND DIED MANY YEARS AGO, LEAVING HER TO RAISE FIVE CHILDREN. SHE IS A GRANDMOTHER OF ELEVEN.

SATURDAY NIGHT AT OMA'S

Ingrid Andor

y brother and I scramble to the top of the immaculate first-floor landing of my grandmother's huge thirteen-flat apartment building. Clomp, clomp, clomp up the carpeted stairs with Mommy and Daddy close behind, anxious to begin their evening alone together. By the time we reach the first door on the right, twelve steps up exactly, it swings open wide to reveal Oma—our beautiful, strong, blond-haired, blue-eyed grandmother, framed in the doorway, holding out her arms and calling to us in delight.

"Meine Engelskinder," she calls out with glee. And my brother and I each

get a turn being smothered to her breast and getting the repeating cheek kiss. First one loud smacker to the right. Then another to the left. Again to the right. Yet again to the left. Here we go again to the right—but wait. Careful now. We're getting so close to the ear. Pow! Pop! A deafening, explosive smooch in the ear and now I will sit in a wind tunnel for a while, waiting for my hearing to come back. I watch Oma's lips move soundlessly and see her beaming down at me with that indisguisable look of delight, pink color in her cheeks, a sparkle to those bright blue eyes.

Engelskind, literally translated from the German, means much more than "grand-child." It means "child of the angels." And that's exactly how I feel when I am with my Oma. Somehow I am elevated, larger than life, and infinitely more appreciated, extra-special, supercalifragilisticexpialidocious—just like Julie Andrews used to sing in *Mary Poppins.*

"Come, eat something. What can I get you? Let's look in the kitchen." It doesn't matter that we have just eaten dinner with our parents. Oma's refrigerator and pantry cupboards are always well stocked with pop, ice cream, cookies, crackers, and chips. I especially like the almond-studded windmill cookies, crisp on the teeth with the taste of nutmeg and ginger on the tongue.

Later, we sit on the pull-out couch in the living room that will convert to our bed, and watch television, usually *Get Smart* with Barbara Felden as Agent 99 and Don Adams as the bumbling secret agent Max. Oma makes popcorn and I watch the light from the TV flash out from the screen, illuminating the wide-open-mouthed, snoring face of my grandfather, sitting in his easy chair with his thick gray ceramic beer stein slipping out of his hands. With smooth, practiced movement, Oma puts the popcorn on the coffee table before us and turns around to pull the stein out of his fingers and right it on the little lamp table beside him. She turns back to join us without even a backward glance.

I am sprawled out lengthwise on the couch now, feeling the rough crocheted bro-cade from the pillow cover on the back of my neck. Oma sits on the opposite end of the couch, putting my feet in her lap. "*Kitzel mich, Oma. Kitzel mich* ['tickle me']," I say.

And as she does all the many times I ask, she removes my socks and begins to stroke the bottom of my feet. It tickles in that delicious way that sends shivers to my head, circling my ears, but mostly it feels very comforting. Oma's large, hardworking veiny hands—hands that can renovate an empty apartment in a day and a half—are warm and soothing to the touch. I begin to drift away, my feet warm and cuddly and tickly in her lap, sleeping the sleep that only a child of the angels can.

INGRID ANDOR, FORTY-TWO, OF THE NOT-SO-RARE BREED OF AVOWED CORPORATE DROPOUTS, IS A WRITER/POET RESIDING IN EVANSTON, ILLINOIS. SHE IS CURRENTLY AT WORK ON A BOOK OF CREATIVE NONFICTION CONCERNING HER FAMILY'S POST–WORLD WAR II REFUGEE AND IMMIGRANT EXPERIENCES AND FINDS SOLACE IN THE SPONTANEOUS RUSH OF CREATING PASSIONATE POEMS, THREE OF WHICH WERE PUBLISHED IN 1997 BY TENACITY PRESS IN AN ANTHOLOGY CALLED *COURAGEOUS JOURNEYS*.

I REMEMBER MAMA

Diana Lee

She leans back in her simple throne: The high-backed chair at the head of the kitchen table goes unchallenged. She views the hum of activity around her, as a queen bee would survey her hives.

They are all here today. The adults, after feasting on a heavy meal of pasta, have settled into soft chairs. They converse with her in an amusing blend of Italian and English. The children, with stubborn spaghetti sauce still clinging to the corners of their mouths, squirm with delight as their rosy cheeks are pinched and their plump bottoms playfully slapped.

She sits enraptured. The silky white hair contrasts powerfully with her deeply creviced olive features. Today she is truly majestic . . . a matriarch whose authority is second to none. Her hands, ripened to antiquity, having diapered generations, lie regally in her ample lap.

Her round body fits snugly in the chair. It was a strong body, but now weary from standing against the winds of age. Her abundant bosom cushions the head of a tired child. It has absorbed a lifetime of tears.

There is wisdom about her. It is something not found in books but accumulated through the days and minutes of a lifetime. Her knowledge lies, like the pages of a lengthy novel, in her memory. The heartwarming stories of that novel are open to anyone with the patience to listen. You will be enthralled by the sunshine memories of Italy and the star-kissed dreams of a new life in America. There are hopes and disappointments, defeats and glories. There are births and deaths, loves and hates; all are recalled in a lighthearted poetry.

She rises now and receives the attention of all. There is an aroma of fresh-brewed espresso and anisette in the air. She moves carefully. Her plump body is almost one with

her short legs. She makes her way to the table and cuts the first slice of cake. The glittering flames of ninety-six candles reveal tears in the eyes of everyone present. Tears that remember all the birthdays gone by. Tears that are leaping into the future, already cherishing the remaining few birthdays that may come.

DIANA LEE, FIFTY-TWO, RECEIVED AN M.A.W. IN WRITING FROM MANHATTAN- VILLE COLLEGE. HER SHORT STORY "HOLLY'S FOLLY" RECEIVED HONORABLE MENTION IN *THE SHORT STORY DIGEST*.

Rosalia Boccellato

GRAND-MOTHER

SUBSTITUTES

ESTHER PETERSON: MY ELEANOR

Elayne Clift

 sther Peterson was a champion of women's rights, a pioneer in the consumer movement, and an icon for organized labor. She rose from her humble Utah beginnings to become the first woman lobbyist for the AFL-CIO, where she was assigned to a young senator named John F. Kennedy. She headed the Women's Bureau when Kennedy later became president, served as Assistant Secretary of Labor during the Johnson administration, and as Special Advisor to President Jimmy Carter. In her eighties, she became a United Nations envoy during the first Clinton administration.

I met Esther because of our mutual work on behalf of women and consumers. We bonded over the saving of Val Kil, Eleanor Roosevelt's beloved home in Hyde Park, New York. We nourished the friendship that developed between us despite a difference in our ages of more than thirty-five years. Esther was the grandmother I never knew, the mother lost to mental illness, my mentor and my muse.

"Oh, my dear," she would say when I shared my writing. "I am mightily moved!" When I was discouraged, she urged me on. When I ranted over the political realities of our time, she lamented with me in violent agreement. When I wanted advice, she gave it freely. And when I simply sought a quiet soul mate, she was that too.

When she became too infirm to go out for ethnic food with me, I would go to her house, a bottle of chilled Chardonnay in my bag. We would sit together in her bedroom or den, reminiscing, sharing, dreaming. She would talk about her beloved husband, Oliver, who died in 1972. We discussed parenting, politics, sex, religion, books, and fantasy trips on the Orient Express or banana boats in Brazil. We mourned the loss of our sisters and explored sibling rivalry. We spoke of death and grief, of the quality of life and the demise of civilization. We told off-color jokes. We gossiped.

During one of my visits, I felt so graced by the joy of this great woman's friendship that I wept. "You are my Eleanor," I told her then, quietly, and she wept too. I knew how much she revered Mrs. Roosevelt, with whom she had worked.

Esther came to my home for Passover Seder each year. My husband and I attended her ninetieth birthday celebration. When she was inducted into the National Women's Hall of Fame in Seneca, New York, I was there. But for me, the special days were those I spent in the cool quiet of her home, just being ourselves, together.

The life she led was an inspiration to many. The relationship we shared was her precious, private, and generous gift to me. I feel blessed to have called her friend.

ELAYNE CLIFT, FIFTY-FIVE, TEACHES IN THE SCHOOL OF PUBLIC HEALTH AT YALE UNIVERSITY AND IN THE ADULT DEGREE PROGRAM AT VERMONT COLLEGE. HER LATEST WORK, A COLLECTION OF SHORT STORIES CALLED *CRONING TALES* (OGN PUBLICATIONS, 1996), WAS DEDICATED TO ESTHER PETERSON.

TINT

Suzanne Nielsen

llen lived next door to Aunt Lil, whose house I went to whenever my mother tired of me, which seemed to happen all the time. I think Ellen was older than Aunt Lil, and Aunt Lil was the oldest person I knew. Aunt Lil didn't like Ellen much because she was Swedish. She told me that Swedes don't keep house and they are stingy.

Ellen shared her coconut and cocoa with me every Sunday evening, hardly what I would call stingy. Our Sunday evenings together revolved around watching *Walt Disney* on her television, in living color. I would always arrive early so I could watch the NBC peacock spread its wings, a different color for each feather spread. Ellen would fiddle around with some of the knobs and change the color a bit as the peacock became a rainbow of color; making it more green or red, what she called "tint." She told me that that colorful peacock was supposed to be the boy peacock, that in nature things were that way. The males were beautiful, and the females were bland and more subdued. She said that was only true of birds, however, and I was much prettier than Kenny who lived across the street. I asked her if I was prettier than my brother Lawrence, because Aunt Lil liked him best and I couldn't figure out why. She said of course I was. I believed her because she never asked Lawrence to come over and watch *Walt Disney* in living color.

Every Sunday evening, at a few minutes before six P.M., I would run out Aunt Lil's back door, jump the fence, take three steps at a time, and, like magic, I would enter Ellen's wonderful world of living color. I didn't care if Aunt Lil thought my quick way of getting to Ellen's wasn't ladylike because Ellen said it was just as important to be a kid as it was to be a lady. Ellen thought it was amazing how much speed I had in my stride, and said she wished she was a kid instead of a lady. I thought she was both, and that's how I wanted to be when I got old enough to be a lady.

Ellen would always have hot cocoa on the stove and shredded coconut for us to eat. I would get to use a plate with a turkey on it for my coconut so I wouldn't get it all over the floor. Ellen didn't have a dog, and she said she was just a particularly clean Swede. I would dent the couch cushions with my body, making it comfortable, just for me.

Then Ellen would wink at me with one eye. I knew this meant she liked me. She taught me how to wink like that with one eye. She said she learned how to wink when she was a kid, that kids and ladies alike could wink at one another if they felt like it. I winked at her from then on, during every station break of *Walt Disney*.

So, there it was, the start of our event. There was the peacock. There were the beautiful colors, and there was Ellen introducing me once again to this thing called tint. Tinkerbell waved her wand, and with every blink of both eyes, a new color of fireworks would appear. This was the life: sitting here with Ellen, eating coconut on turkey plates, sipping hot chocolate like ladies did their coffee, and watching something so beautiful as living color.

When I'd return to Aunt Lil's, she'd ask what Ellen and I did. I lied every Sunday night to her about that. Sometimes I'd say we played Chinese checkers, sometimes I'd tell her we painted flowers on Ellen's doorknobs with tempera paints. No matter what I told her we did, she didn't act surprised, which is the response I wanted. If she knew Ellen and I watched television for an hour, she'd never let me go back for more. She thought watching color television would ruin my eyes and make me unable to have babies, even if I sat far away.

I could go on and on to Aunt Lil about what Ellen and I did, if need be, but there was never a need for me to give any more information. I'd go on and on in my head though, thinking how much fun it would be to paint those flowers on Ellen's doorknobs, trying not to drip any paint on the floor, yet knowing even though she was a particularly clean Swede, she'd wink at me first, then wipe up the drip.

SUZANNE NIELSEN, FORTY-TWO, GREW UP ON ST. PAUL'S EAST SIDE, A WORKING-CLASS COMMUNITY THAT HAS PROVIDED THE INSPIRATION FOR MUCH OF HER WORK. MS. NIELSEN GRADUATED FROM METRO STATE UNIVERSITY AND IS CURRENTLY WORKING ON A MASTER'S DEGREE AT HAMLINE UNIVERSITY. SHE CONTINUES TO RESIDE IN THE TWIN CITIES WITH HER FAMILY.

THE GETTING BETTER PART

Murph Henderson

 was five and chasing imaginary butterflies in our living room when I first met Joanne. My mother had just died. It took my father thirty seconds to decide to ask Joanne and her husband to move in with us. As the story goes, she turned to her husband when our front door had closed behind them and said, "We have to help these people."

Joanne was a wise twenty-six. She fed me peanut-butter-fluffernutter sandwiches and baked me my first pizza. She bathed me every night, except for the night of our fire when she drove two cars, one after the other, from the burning garage. And she let me watch each time she stood before the mirror to create her masterful hairdo: long tresses teased into a rat's nest, the top layer combed smooth over the tangle, two dangling ringlets just in front of her ears, and the whole arrangement sprayed with Miss Breck. The prettiest almost-mom in the neighborhood.

Joanne's listening ear was the most attentive and confidential I have ever known. When I went away to college, she phoned me every Sunday night, despite her own struggles to meet a doctoral student's deadlines, as well as the needs of her young family and employer. Years later, when I was ill and alone in Philadelphia, she arranged for a gourmet food shop to deliver my meals, then phoned each night until I was well.

When *I* was twenty-six, doctors diagnosed Joanne with the same disease that had killed my mother. I stored my belongings, rented a car, and drove 700 miles to climb into bed with her. "Are we getting better or are we dying?" I asked. "I want to help you do whichever it is."

"Let's work on the getting better part," she said.

Surgeries. Chemotherapy. Meditation and prayer. Joanne took Chinese herbs, powdered shark cartilage, and essence of Venus flytrap. I was her companion through all but her last treatment, administered in Germany. I pictured Joanne there on a sunny Alpine mountaintop. She wore a blue dress, billowed by the wind. She stood with her spine straight and her arms outstretched ready to embrace any challenge from her cliff edge.

I speak to the winds sometimes now and hope that she hears me. "You climbed some mountain," I tell her. "Thanks for teaching me so much about mountain climbing. Thanks for letting yours be the one door I could walk through without knocking. Thanks for claiming a daughter not even yours and helping to make her whole."

OHIO FARM GIRL JOANNE AUGSPURGER STRENGTHENED MURPH HENDERSON FOR MORE THAN TWO DECADES. JOANNE ALSO RAISED TWO SONS, LAUNCHED A WOMEN'S CENTER, AND COUNSELED EXECUTIVES DEVASTATED BY JOB LOSS BEFORE HER DEATH IN 1993. MURPH, NOW THIRTY-THREE, WRITES FICTION IN NEW YORK.

CONVERSATION WITH FLORENCE

Miriam Fabbri

lorence Bridgeman was in her early eighties when I met her. She and her husband, Odie, were our neighbors when I lived in the country on a commune in southern Illinois. The farm where they lived had been settled by Odie's father in the 1800s.

I am in the holler beside the fallen giant tree. Florence is there. I ask her, "What will it take for me to get over this hurt and be happy in my life again? What will I do? . . ."

"Aw, honey," she says, "there ain't nothin' you can do—life jist is—like the creek. It rises and falls and you cain't do nothin' about it. You watch it carry things away—sometimes you get stuck in it—but it keeps on shiftin' and

Florence
Bridgeman

movin'. Sometimes it's such a little dried up old trickle that you think it ain't no danger and you can tame it, til it rises up again, swollen with rain, and washes away everything you thought was stick or solid.

"You watch it flow, trickle, rage. You jist watch and go on about your business. Can them peaches, freeze them berries, and you can eat them all winter long. And in the spring, you plant again—and work each season 'cuz they are.

"Life is busy, always changin'. Be curious. Life will fill you."

MIRIAM FABBRI RECEIVED HER MASTER OF FINE ARTS FROM SOUTHERN ILLINOIS UNIVERSITY. HER WORK HAS APPEARED IN *MS.* MAGAZINE AND *NEW WOMAN'S SURVIVAL SOURCEBOOK.* SHE HAS DESIGNED AND PRODUCED GREETING CARDS AND POSTERS THROUGH OPEN WINDOW CREATIONS. MIRIAM CURRENTLY RESIDES IN BERKELEY, CALIFORNIA, AND TEACHES ART TO MIDDLE-SCHOOL STUDENTS.

MISS "H"

Cherise Wyneken

iss Hamburger, my English teacher at Acalanes Union High School in Lafayette, California, during the 1940s, was affectionately called Miss "H" by her students. We girls loved her most for her role as leader of the extra curricular activity modern dance (à la Isadora Duncan).

A lovely woman, with striking black hair and a lithe slender body, she taught us how to move ours gracefully, to hear stories and see movements in music, to create and choreograph. We gained self-confidence through her acceptance and encouragement as we performed before an audience at spring and fall concerts. Our appreciation of music grew as we danced to "Hungarian Rhapsody No. 2," "Go Down, Moses," or Tchaikovsky's "Sleeping Beauty Waltz." Dance brought aspects of our subconscious out from behind our ego masks and let them move and be exposed.

But it was in her English class that I learned the most valuable lesson she offered. "I'm going to read you an article on anti-Semitism," she said to the class one day. "Then I want you to write a paper discussing it." I had never heard that term before and didn't have a clue as to what it meant. The article spoke of Hitler's aggrandizement of blond, blue-eyed Aryans above other races; of pogroms, ghettos, and discrimination involving Jews. I had been brought up in a Christian setting, sent to Sunday school and studied Bible stories. To me the word *Jew* simply meant God's people in Old Testament times. Why should they be treated badly?

That day, seated in a wooden desk in a small classroom, my eyes were opened to the horror of racism. My innocent world of family, friends, music, and dance was suddenly expanded to include sounds of suffering from people outside my little circle. I strongly defended the Jews in my essay.

Just as dance brought out my feelings, Miss "H"'s introduction to prejudice was a stepping stone to inclusiveness. Her lesson, assimilated at a formative age, helped me deal with relationships in creative ways. Ultimately, I gained an international family: an African-American son-in-law, a Mexican-American son-in-law, a Jewish daughter-in-law, and even an Episcopalian (I was brought up Lutheran). Miss "H" wove patterns of tolerance into my life, allowing me to celebrate and appreciate the variety in my expanding family.

As I write this, Miss "H" is in her late nineties, very much alive, still dancing!

CHERISE WYNEKEN IS A SIXTY-NINE-YEAR-OLD WIFE, MOTHER, GRANDMOTHER, FORMER ELEMENTARY-SCHOOL TEACHER, AND PUBLISHED FREELANCE WRITER OF PROSE AND POETRY—ADULT AND JUVENILE. HER WORK HAS APPEARED IN MANY JOURNALS, INCLUDING *BLACK CHILD*, *PALO ALTO REVIEW*, *THEMA*, *EARTH'S DAUGHTERS*, *MATURE YEARS*, *SOUTH FLORIDA PARENTING*, *LUTHERAN WOMEN*, AND OTHERS.

MY FIRST ENCOUNTER WITH A FEMINIST

Ruth Cash-Smith

hen I first heard Lillie Margaret Lazaruk's voice, I thought of magnolia trees and Spanish moss. My second thought was that it had to be a fake accent, but as soon as I met her, I knew that wasn't the case. There wasn't a single phony thing about this new college administrator at my urban ghetto community college in the mid-1970s.

She was maybe fifty, tall and rangy with short brown hair. She wore sedate clothes, mostly in grays and tans, nothing that screamed. Ever. Harsh New England winters, so different from the warmer Southern climes she was used to, often tormented her lungs, so all she had to do was cough or complain of a scratchy throat, and I would urge herbal teas and home remedies on her, anything to soothe her discomfort. Awed by her power, I attached myself to her, first as a student worker and then later as one of her many protégées.

Beneath her silky Southern voice lay a will of feminist steel. While other women may have given up the battle for women's rights, Lillie Margaret grew ever more invigorated, butting heads with stagnant white-male bureaucrats in college administration, calling attention to the old-boy closed network of power lunches and workouts at the health club. Hers was a voice that refused to be silenced.

Through student efforts, money was raised for a Women's Center at the community college. And Lillie Margaret was chosen as the director. She, along with an amazingly diverse group of students, lobbied for an on-site child-care center, Women's History Month celebrations, and—scariest of all to the embattled men—equal pay for equal work.

Tireless in her work to achieve equality for all people, she made remarkably rational arguments against whatever status quo the men were busy defending. With her awesome ability for strategic thinking, she surged ahead in winning victories that improved the lives of women students at my alma mater.

Somehow in spite of a demanding career of her own, she also carved time for her husband and son, and used any free time to back countless efforts aimed at improving women's lives on every front.

With her encouragement, I, along with many others whom she mentored, pursued degrees in higher-education administration. Slowly, in our own ways, we carried on the fight to make women's voices heard and heeded in colleges. In my first position I'd often feel isolated and alone, but if I listened intently, I seemed to hear Lillie Margaret, like a guardian angel, whispering her hard-won wisdoms in my ear. Often I relied on the secret arsenal of weapons I'd seen her wield and made much-needed changes in my own college. And during the next two decades of my career, I always made time to mentor a female student, offering whatever I could to help her achieve her potential, as Lillie Margaret had done for me.

RUTH CASH-SMITH LIVES NEAR THE LAST TOWN IN COASTAL MAINE. HER ARTICLES AND ESSAYS HAVE APPEARED IN *THE WRITER, GOOD OLD DAYS, DOWN EAST, COLLEGE MONTHLY, SAN DIEGO FAMILY PRESS,* AND *REFLECTIONS ON MAINE.* CURRENTLY SHE IS AT WORK ON *HALLELUJAH JUNCTION,* A FICTIONAL WORK ABOUT THE UNDERBELLY OF LIFE IN A SMALL MIDWESTERN TOWN, WHERE NOTHING IS AS IT FIRST APPEARS. DURING THE VERY LONG MAINE WINTERS, SHE TEACHES BUSINESS-COMMUNICATION CLASSES IN SOUTHEAST ASIA.

A BRIDGE TO
MY SOUL
Maria Isabel Viana

fter graduating from college, I rented a room in the New England home of an eighty-nine-year-old woman. Each evening around suppertime, I'd join Emily in the kitchen where we'd talk for hours. Emily narrated many interesting stories in her soft, slightly hoarse voice on topics ranging from the women's suffrage movement to her having to learn her husband's business overnight after his death. I heard words that revealed Emily's strength and how rich she allowed her experiences to make her.

Emily's stories were often spiced with a supernatural quality that made me question what I accepted as reality. One evening Emily told me of her efforts to keep the pipes from freezing and bursting in her late husband's office on her first Christmas Eve without him. The furnace had gone off. Unable to keep the pipes from freezing, she struggled with the decision to leave the office. At that decisive moment, somebody knocked on the door. A man she'd never seen before and would never see again walked in and began to give her instructions.

They spent the night rinsing the pipes with boiling water. On Christmas morning, as the temperature rose above freezing, Emily's guardian angel bid her farewell. As the stranger reached for the door, Emily asked, "Who are you?"

The man grinned and said, "Santa Claus."

Emily said that was when she started accepting the mysteries of her life as gifts.

Because of Emily I started believing facts I couldn't prove with my five senses. Emily's stories stretched my mind, expanding its limits to embrace new truths.

One morning in midsummer, I lay on the floor after a run, my legs up against a wall to get the blood back to my thighs. I didn't think of anything as I lay relaxed on the cool wooden boards. Suddenly, the strongest feeling I've ever had of grandeur, of sacredness flooded me, and for the first time in my life I recognized my soul. It was as tangible as the furniture around me, and I could feel it snug inside the shell that was my body. I felt grateful to Emily for all the experiences she'd shared with me, which prepared me to live through that wonderful moment and to accept it without analysis.

A year later I moved south but never lost touch with Emily. Two years after we'd met, I called her to say I'd be in New England the following week. She sounded as cheerful as ever, but when she said, "I have something to tell you when you arrive," a pang tightened my chest, as if my intuition had heard more than what had been said.

Emily died the day I traveled to Massachusetts. She left me the inheritance of moments of love and friendship I can recall for the rest of my life. She also left me my connection with my soul, by putting me in touch with my spiritual essence.

MARIA ISABEL VIANA, THIRTY-ONE, WAS BORN AND RAISED IN BRAZIL. TEN YEARS AGO, SHE MOVED TO THE UNITED STATES. SHE LIVES IN GEORGIA.

YOUR GRANDMOTHER
MEMORIES

Perhaps the stories in this book prompted personal reflection. Use the following pages to record your favorite grandmother memories. The following questions may provide a starting point for you to write your own grandmother story—or stories!

What is your fondest memory of your grandmother?
What is the greatest lesson she taught you?
How has this lesson affected your life?
How do you share what you learned from your grandmother with others?

_____

_____

_____

_____

_____

Love bears all things, believes all things, hopes all things.

I COR. 13:7

_We can do no great things—only small things with
great love._

Where there is love, there's no lack.

RICHARD BROME

How vast a memory has Love!

SAPPHO

ACKNOWLEDGMENTS

NO CREATIVE PROJECT comes into existence without the love and support of family and friends.

When I took a year's sabbatical in Chicago to focus on *Gifts from Our Grandmothers,* my parents, Frances and Santino Dovi, cheered me on rather than telling me that I was crazy. My sister, Maria Stankiewicz, spent many hours, including vacation time, editing stories. My brother-in-law Bob, and nephews Chris and Andrew, exhibited great patience and love. My brother, John, and his family, Karen, Allison, and Matthew, provided me with lots of "you go, girl's."

Kay Adams offered valuable coaching at the beginning stages of the book. The "home team"—Steve Anderson, Joel Fotinos, Jackie June, Doug Krug, Sheri Krug, Richard James, Verity Lehr, Linda Lundborg, Mary Dean Marshall, Sara Noel, and Debra Whitaker—provided encouragement via e-mail and phone calls.

My best friend, Karyn Kedar, has seen and brought out the best in me for twenty-five years. She opened her heart and home to help me complete this book. Her wonderful children, Talia, Shiri, and Ilan, adopted me as an aunt and offered me an advanced course in flexibility and playfulness.

Onnie Baldwin and Ingrid Andor graciously took time away from their own writing projects to critique stories.

A whole family of angels crossed my path in Chicago. Lisa Marks Fisher spent hours listening to stories and offering editorial assistance; Susan Marks Venturi shared her ideas and contacts with me; Roz and Jim Marks generously provided a beautiful place for me to live and work in downtown Chicago during a critical period in the book's development.

Rev. Jane Kopp of the First Divine Science Church in Denver, Colorado, and Rev. Pat Williamson of Unity on the North Shore in Evanston, Illinois, offered an abun-

221

dance of love and spiritual support.

It was a joy to work with my agent, Victoria Sanders, and my editor, Rachel Kahan. I appreciate their patience, responsiveness, wisdom, and guidance.

The work of Julia Cameron, Susan Page, and Barbara Sher inspired and instructed me before and during this project.

I lovingly honor the memory of my friend Darrel Matteson, who believed this book would reach completion because it was motivated by love.

Many thanks to all the women who took the time to share their grandmother stories. I'm also grateful to the women who provided the inspiration for these stories.

ABOUT THE AUTHOR

CAROL DOVI makes her home in Denver, Colorado. A midlife crisis and love of her grandmother created the impetus for this book. Carol works as an admissions representative for a proprietary school.